POLITICAL PORTRAITS

POLITICAL PORTRAITS

SECOND SERIES

BY

CHARLES WHIBLEY

Essay Index Reprint Series

 BOOKS FOR LIBRARIES PRESS
FREEPORT, NEW YORK

First Published 1923
Reprinted 1970

STANDARD BOOK NUMBER:
8369-1734-0

LIBRARY OF CONGRESS CATALOG CARD NUMBER:
76-117859

PRINTED IN THE UNITED STATES OF AMERICA

CONTENTS

PORTRAITS

PORTRAITS

A

BOLINGBROKE

I

DR. JOHNSON in his Dictionary gives these words as an example of irony : 'Bolingbroke was a holy man.' The example fails from whichever point it be viewed. Irony, to be sure, is something more subtle than a direct opposite, and the 'unholiness' of Bolingbroke, which Johnson would have us take for granted, is the result of an old and deeply rooted prejudice. No sooner had Henry St. John brought peace to England by the Treaty of Utrecht, than all his enemies began with one accord to malign him. 'Chesterfield says,' wrote Bolingbroke many years afterwards, 'I have made a coalition of Whig, Tory, Trimmer, Jacobite against myself. Be it so. I have Truth, that is stronger than all of them, on my side, and in her company, and avowed by her, I have more satisfaction than their applause and their favour could give me.' Bolingbroke was unduly sanguine. The truth takes an unconscionable time to establish herself, and even yet lags behind the swift slanders of the Whigs. To blacken the character of Bolingbroke was laid by Walpole as a solemn duty upon all his friends. Walpole's fribble son, for whom Bolingbroke was 'this incendiary,' loses no opportunity, which malice and falsehood might suggest, of insulting the memory of his father's great opponent.   Macaulay, for whom the Whig tradition was a pious trust, denounces Boling-broke as 'a brilliant knave,' at the very moment when he applauds the authors of the peace.   In all the tabernacles, where the pure doctrine of the Whigs is still preached, the malevolence of Walpole persists. Nor have the Tories been eager to rally to the defence of their champion.   The admiring eloquence of Disraeli has had far less effect upon the opinion of the Tories than the theological rancour of Samuel Johnson. 'Sir,' said the doctor, when Bolingbroke's works were published by David Mallet—'Sir, he was a scoundrel and a coward : a scoundrel for discharging a blunder-buss against religion and morality ; a coward, because he had not resolution to fire it off himself, but left half-a-crown to a beggarly Scotchman to draw the trigger after his death.'   Truth, after two centuries, is still on Bolingbroke's side, slow-footed though she be, and since the Whigs' hold upon history is already loosened, we may yet see some measure of justice done to the fame and character of a great man.

Henry St. John, Viscount Bolingbroke, was born when Charles II. was on the throne.   Of a noble and wealthy family, he carried in his veins the mixed blood of Cavalier and Roundhead.   By a strange irony, he who was destined to lead the Church Party and presently to prove a scourge for the orthodox was guided in his first steps by Daniel Burgess, a fanatical and humorous Presbyterian, and was held so strictly in the leading-strings of Dissent that he was obliged, as he says himself, 'while yet a boy, to read over the commentaries of Dr. Manton, whose pride it was to have made a hundred and nineteen sermons on the hundred and nineteenth psalm.' That he happily outgrew this early training has been for his detractors a stubborn cause of offence, as though perpetual loyalty to the lessons of the schoolroom was the first and abiding duty of a man. A sojourn at Eton, which mitigated the severity of his early training, was an excellent prelude to the Grand Tour. And when St. John set out to visit France and Italy he was well equipped to profit by what he saw and heard. The letters which he sent from abroad to Sir William Trumbull,[1] a statesman forty years older than himself, are saved from pedantry only by a boyish enthusiasm. A first sight of France, in May 1698, convinces him that she ' has all the melancholy marks of war and absolute government, which are two of God's sharpest judgments, and which there is but one more can equal and that is a tyrannical Hierarchy ; for I believe you will permit me to say that the servants of Heaven are the worst masters.' Young as he was, he did not scruple to give Trumbull good advice, to regret his absence from public employment, and to remind him of Tully's admirable sentence : *non nobis solum, sed*

[1] These letters are to be found in the Easthampstead Papers, published by the Historical Manuscripts Commission.

etiam patriæ nati sumus. Having chosen Trumbull
for a pattern, he assures him amiably that, ' being
resolved to draw as good a copy as he can after so
excellent an original, he applies himself to that study
in which he (Trumbull) became so perfect a master.'
In other words, he devotes himself to the study of
Roman Law, and piously deplores the decline of the
Roman spirit. ' There was a time, sir,' writes he
with a boyish pomp which he presently discarded,
' when their divine spirit (if I might use the expression)
shed its influence on us ; there was a time when *dulce
et decorum est pro patria mori* was imprinted on our
hearts, when zeal for liberty, courage, integrity, and
virtue were as much in fashion as the contrary vices
are now.'

Wherever he goes he sends to his elderly friend such
news as he thinks will be welcome to him. He has
all the contempt of youth for the learning of Italy,
whose ' knowledge serves so little to the advancement
of a man that there is scarce any one who aims at it.'
Not even the name and fame of Magliabecchi appal
him. Believing him to be a man of erudition, he
found when he met him ' an old, vain, senseless pedant,
a great devourer of books without any method or digest
in what he reads, a kind of Bethlem character, one that
is always busy without proposing to himself any end.'
Here we have a St. John who is something of a scholar,
eagerly intent to display his learning, and who yet
foreshadows faintly what Bolingbroke is to be. And
that which he brought back from the Grand Tour,

more valuable than the mastery of French or the knowledge of foreign lands, was the habit of study and love of books, which died in him only with his death. ' I have some of St. Evremond's works before me,' he writes to Trumbull in 1699 from Milan, ' and may apply that in general which he says in particular of an orator, that before a man ventures to produce himself in the world, he must have by reading enrich his mind, and not pretend to spend before he has got an estate.' St. John could not have drawn his wisdom from a better source than St. Evremond. They were *honnêtes gens* both, scholars and men of affairs, who knew the grief of exile, and could bear with a good courage all the blows that fortune aimed at them.

Meanwhile, he was mingling with a love of study a love of life. His eager, apprehensive mind seized upon pleasure with the same greed wherewith it seized upon knowledge. He was eminent in dissipation in a dissipated age. He is said to have taken for his models Alcibiades and Petronius, and he has suffered ever since less for the vices in which he indulged than for the frankness with which he proclaimed them. Rochester had been dead less than twenty years when Bolingbroke came upon the town, and that man of wayward genius was still an example to the golden and lettered youth. But the old man, who assured his biographer that he saw St. John and another of his companions run drunk and naked through the Park, was making a theft upon the past, and ascribing to St. John the grosser sins which marked the restoration

of Charles ii. The lover of the famous Miss Gumley
had, surely, something majestic in his frivolity, and
liberal though he was in intrigue, disdained to outrage
the laws of elegance imposed upon his generation. He
was, indeed, the highest expression of the age of Anne.
In him wit and gallantry went hand in hand. He
was Mirabell in action, and might well have been a
member of that society whose conversation inspired
The Way of the World, a society which, Congreve says
in his letter of dedication to the Earl of Montague,
' was so well worthy of you in your retirement last
summer from the town.'

As I have said, he did not allow pleasure to interrupt the graver business of his life. ' The love of
study,' he wrote himself, with perfect truth, ' and the
desire of knowledge, were what I felt all my life ; and
though my genius, unlike the dæmon of Socrates,
whispered so softly, that very often I heard him not
in the hurry of these passions with which I was trans-
ported, yet some calmer hours there were, and in them
I harkened to him.' In a passage in his Essay on the
Spirit of Patriotism, he has made with the eloquent
passion of regret an apology for his own career. ' The
service of our country,' he writes, ' is no chimerical
but a real duty. . . . Superior talents and superior
rank among our fellow-creatures, whether acquired
by birth or by the course of accidents and the success
of their own industry, are noble prerogatives. Shall
he who possesses them repine at the obligation they
lay him under of passing his whole life in the noblest

occupation of which human nature is capable ? . . .
To be driven from hence by successful tyranny, by
loss of health or of parts, or by the force of accidents,
is to be degraded in such a manner as to deserve pity
and not to incur blame ; but to degrade ourselves, to
descend voluntarily and by choice from the highest to
a lower, perhaps to the lowest rank of the sons of
Adam ; to abandon the government of men for that
of hounds and horses, the care of a kingdom for that
of a parish, and a scene of great and generous efforts in
public life for one of trifling amusements and low
cares, of sloth, of idleness, what is it, my Lord ? I
had rather your Lordship should name it than I.'

It was, in truth, tyranny, and not his own fault,
which drove him from the service of his country.
Much as he delighted in trifling amusements, he never
was their slave, and it was his earliest, as it was his
lasting if frustrated ambition, to engage in public
business. No sooner was he married than he was
urgent to find employment at home or abroad. They
who find monstrosity in every step of his career have
been busy in condemning his treatment of his wife.
They have condemned it without evidence. It is true
that he made light of marriage, with his customary
irony, when it came about. 'That I was married
last Thursday,' he wrote to Trumbull, on Monday,
26th May 1701, 'is a trifling piece of news, and yet it
is the only thing I know of that has happened since
you left London' ; and thereafter he quotes in a spirit
of gaiety, *vixi puellis nuper idoneus* and the rest of it.

His wife was Frances, daughter of Sir Henry Winch-combe, and a direct descendant of Jack of Newbury. With her he kept house for many years, both in Golden Square and in the country. We see little more of her than an amiable shadow cast upon the page of history. She won the difficult heart of Swift, who was constant in attachment to her. When he took leave of her on 10th April 1711, she 'gave him strict charge to take care of the Secretary in her absence ; said she had none to trust but me ; and the poor creature's tears came fresh in her eyes.' There is no proof here of indifference, and when a few months later Swift visited St. John in Berkshire, he painted a pleasant picture, strangely at variance with that which other artists have given us. 'Mr. Secretary,' writes Swift, 'was a perfect country gentleman at Buckle-bury ; he inquired after the wheat in such a field ; he smoked tobacco with one or two neighbours ; he went to visit his hounds, and knew all their names ; he and his lady saw me to my chamber just in the country fashion.' And then comes Voltaire, with the jest he is determined not to lose. 'Seven thousand guineas a year, my girls, and all for us !' Thus a woman of the town is said by Voltaire to have welcomed St. John's appointment as Secretary of State. I prefer the evidence of Swift, at once intimate and credible.

And one good thing marriage did for St. John. It turned his mind, as I have said, to public business. He very soon discovered that, though in time his estate would be very considerable, yet he 'must expect for a great while to be in low circumstances, unless,' as he told Trumbull, 'I raise 'em myself, and that is what, to you I make nothing a secret, I long to do.' It was not for him to despair or complain. 'You know me well enough, I believe,' he wrote to his friend, 'to find that I have some spirit, and indeed I have too much to sit down easily under a strait fortune.' So when his troubles 'plunged him into a deep melancholy,' Horace, 'like a powerful magician,' came to his aid. And though, happily for him and for England, he was not sent to a post abroad, he threw himself with all his energy into the work of the House of Commons. To that body he had been returned, at the age of one-and-twenty, by Wootton Bassett, and perforce became a strong partisan of the Tories. In the age of Anne none could hope for preferment who did not profess an unquestioning zeal for the success of his party, and of St. John it may be said that, while he played the necessary part with courage and address, he did less violence to the principles he had made his own than any one of them. 'As far as I can recollect,' he wrote to Swift in August 1731, 'my way of thinking has been uniform enough for more than twenty years.' With a clear conscience he might have carried the uniformity still further back. Assuredly, from his first entrance to the House of Commons to his enforced seclusion from that chamber, he remained, so to say, all of one piece.

He first showed his full activity in his reasoned and

reasonable opposition to that cunning device known as
' Occasional Conformity.'   St. John's attitude towards
orthodox theology differed very little from that
which Disraeli was destined to assume.   He had a
single-minded respect for the Church as a part of
the State.   He aimed honestly at statesmanship, and
he thought it no more than his duty, and Swift, always
a devout Churchman, approved his action, to take the
early sacrament at St. James's.   At the same time he
held it a farce, naturally enough, that Dissenters should
make an annual obeisance to the Church for their
private and public profit.   There was no suspicion of
religious intolerance in this action of the Tories.
' The principle of the present Ministry,' said St. John,
' is neither to oppress the Dissenters under pretence
of securing the Establishment, nor to suffer them,
under the specious colour of moderation, to gain spirit
and strength enough to provoke and insult the Church.'
For St. John the debate was important, because it
served to reveal the gift of oratory, which is said to
have been, of all his gifts, the greatest.   Orators, like
actors, write their names in water, and not a scrap of
St. John's eloquence remains to support the general
admiration.   Perhaps it is enough for glory that the
Younger Pitt said that he would rather had heard him
than any of the orators of antiquity.

In 1704 his eloquence was rewarded by the office
of Secretary at War.   That he highly distinguished
himself in these years of England's military glory is
evident.   With a man of genius commanding in the

field, and a statesman at the War Office to support
the army with sympathy and without stint, it would
have been strange, indeed, had our arms not triumphed.
St. John was rare among Ministers in standing by the
General, who might be supposed to understand his
own business, and he may well claim his share in the
victory of Blenheim. In Marlborough he had a
complete trust, and the two men worked together with
a zeal and magnanimity which ensured the defeat of
the French.

St. John enjoyed but a few years of office. A
difference with Godolphin kept him out of Parliament in 1708, and for two years he remained,
willingly, in the seclusion of Bucklebury. He
devoted his leisure to his favourite studies, and
never forgot the debt which he owed to this time of
retirement. When he came back to public affairs,
he was ready to assume the heaviest burden of toil,
and to fight with the courage which never failed him
the enemies of his country at home and abroad. In
1710 he was appointed Secretary of State, and stood
at the zenith of his genius and his charm. A few
months after his appointment Swift painted him in
such colours as seemed to promise him a long and
splendid career. ' I think Mr. St. John,' he wrote
to Stella, ' the greatest young man I ever knew : Wit,
capacity, beauty, quickness of apprehension, good
learning and an excellent taste ; the best orator in the
House of Commons, admirable conversation, good
nature, and good manners ; generous and a despiser

of money.' Nor were St. John's gifts merely spectacular. The same witness who testifies to his wit and beauty testifies also ' to the accomplishments of his mind, which was adorned with the choicest gifts that God hath yet thought fit to bestow upon the children of men,' and greatly marvels at his prodigious application, ' for he would plod whole days and nights, like the lowest clerk in an office.'

No sooner was he Secretary of State than he began to contrive that treaty with France which was at once his glory and his undoing. The task which he imposed upon himself was not easy. He determined upon no less an enterprise than to bring back England from the glamour of Marlborough and of victory. None knew better than he how to distinguish between war and the fruits of war. ' Here let me say,' he wrote in his eighth Letter on History, a vivid piece of autobiography, ' that the glory of taking towns and winning battles is to be measured by the utility that results from those victories. Victories that bring honour to the arms may bring shame to the councils of a nation. To win a battle, to take a town, is the glory of a general and of an army. Of this glory we had a very large share in the course of the war. But the glory of a nation is to proportion the ends she proposes to her interest and her strength ; the means she employs to the ends she proposes, and the vigour she exerts to both.' England had, indeed, thought a great deal of military glory, and very little of the end which she hoped to reach. St. John estimated the cost of

taking Bouchain at seven millions, and he would have
been a clever man who could have measured the
advantage which England had gained from the subsidies lavished, in ceaseless generosity, upon the Allies.

'Ten glorious campaigns are passed,' wrote Swift,.
'and now at last, like the sick man, we are just ex-
piring with all sorts of good symptoms.' Or, to use
another image, when a town was taken by our armies
in Flanders, it was handed over to the Dutch, and we
lit bonfires. The victory was not worth the faggots,
and it was no wonder that the Tory statesman saw
the instant necessity of peace. However, St. John
did not underrate the difficulty or the hazard of his
scheme, nor did he leave any point of the game to be
played by others. In all respects, the peace was a
personal and deliberate achievement. St. John reshaped public opinion, while he contested the Treaty,
article by article, with de Torcy. At his behest, the
Abbé Gaultier and Matthew Prior travelled backwards and forwards between London and Paris. With
his collaboration and guidance, Swift's 'wonder-
working pamphlet' was written. The days spent
at Windsor were not spent in vain ; eleven thousand
copies of that masterpiece of controversy, *The Conduct
of the Allies*, were sold and read in two months, and
Swift uttered no vain boast when he claimed that
it opened the eyes of the nation, half bewitched
against a peace. In 1712 the Treaty of Utrecht was
signed, calm was at last restored to a stricken world,
and St. John was rewarded by a peerage. To-day

nobody will pretend that it was a bad or unnecessary peace. If France were treated with moderation, England could not complain of the benefits which she derived from the tireless wisdom of St. John. The author of the Peace discussed it some years later in his *Letter to Sir William Windham* with an evident satisfaction. He admitted that neither treaties nor negotiations were without faults, some of them due, he confessed, to himself, many others to the opposition which they met at every step. Yet, said he, ' I never look back on this great event, past as it is, without a secret emotion of mind ; when I compare the vastness of the undertaking, and the importance of its success, with the means employed to bring it about, and with those which were employed to traverse it.' To make peace single-handed is a supreme test of skill. To make it with allies ready at every step to hinder and to thwart, is a desperate adventure. And, as St. John deplored, ' each of our allies thought himself entitled to raise his demands to the most extravagant height,' relying upon reckless promises which had been made to them to persuade them to come into or to continue in the war, and boasting, each of them, that he had in truth won the victory.

In the years devoted to the making of the peace, St. John had found in Harley an enemy, who had to be fought at home. That they should ever have been friends is surprising, for they were in all respects the antithesis one of the other. St. John was a man of imagination, who took long views, and had already shaped in his mind a political philosophy. Harley, on the other hand, was timid and vacillating ; a politician who thought he might succeed in playing off friend against foe, or foe against friend. By habit a Tory, he was in temperament a Whig, and though at the outset he dominated St. John by the mere weight of years, St. John presently discerned the inferiority of his mind, and regretted nine years afterwards that in 1710 he 'was weak enough to list again under the conduct of a man of whom nature meant to make a spy or at most a captain of miners ; and whom fortune, in one of her whimsical moods, made a general.' Moreover, in his *Letter to Sir William Windham* he gave a clear expression of the hatred for Harley which, half-hidden, had long consumed him. In a sense a proof of weakness, this passion is easily explained. St. John knew, as Harley also knew in his heart, that he was the better and wiser man ; that he possessed in full measure the qualities of leadership, which Harley lacked. He was supreme in the House of Commons, where Harley's credit ran so low that he was glad to take refuge in the Upper Chamber. Of St. John it may be said, what Disraeli said of Peel, that he played upon the House of Commons as on an old fiddle. 'You know the nature of that assembly,' wrote St. John ; ' they grow, like hounds, fond of the man who shows them game, and by whose halloo they are used to be encouraged.' Harley, never encouraging, was conscious of his defect, and this consciousness made the distance which separated the two men wide and inevitable.

St. John, at any rate, thought that Harley was
doing his best to ruin him in the eyes of the Queen,
and Harley, being a man of affairs, could not endure
quietly the pangs of jealousy. The dark portrait
which St. John, mixing his colours with a fury of
contempt, painted of Harley, must needs be lifelike,
because it seems to reproduce exactly the traits of the
eternal politician. As we look upon it, we can but
acknowledge its familiarity, and say to ourselves that
many another name, set at its foot, would suit as well.
Though Harley (or Oxford as he was then) was the
undisputed chief of the party, he was so indolent that
he negotiated only by fits and starts. ' This man,'
wrote St. John, ' seemed to be sometimes asleep, and
sometimes at play.' While the work of the treaty
was going on, Oxford ' broke now and then a jest,
which savoured of the Inns of Court and the bad
company in which he had been bred,' and left it to
others to make peace with France and to defend the
Tory Party, vulnerable as it was, against the attacks
of the Whigs and its own dissensions. Thus thinking
the worst of everybody, the bubble of his own distrust
and jealousy, he was a man, says St. John, ' who substituted artifice in the place of ability ; who, instead
of leading parties and governing accidents, was eternally agitated backwards and forwards by both ; who
began every day something new, and carried on nothing
to perfection.' How well we know him ! Truly
Harley has not been without his successors, and
Bolingbroke's ancient hatred may be justified by many
a modern instance.

Meanwhile, the hopes of the Tory Party crumbled. If something were not done to regain the public confidence, the Ministers would stand in jeopardy of their lives. At last the long-wished-for security seemed to be at hand. On 27th July 1714, the Queen, not without much persuasion from Mrs. Masham, dismissed Oxford, and St. John, or Bolingbroke as he was then, saw a chance of strengthening the defences of his party against the well-earned resentment of the Whigs. In vain had Oxford been sent about his business. Five days later the Queen died, and there was not a Tory of them all who did not come within the danger of the implacable Walpole. 'What a world it is!' wrote Bolingbroke to Swift, 'and how does fortune banter us!' Truly fortune had bantered them. The Queen's death was the signal to many of instant flight. George i. came to England, not as king of the country, but as the leader of the Whigs, and the Tories knew well that from him and his advisers they might expect neither justice nor fair-play. Swift made his way with what speed he could to Ireland, Oxford was sent to the Tower, and Bolingbroke, partly because he preferred not to lose his head, partly because he 'abhorred Oxford to that degree, that I could not bear to be joined with him in any case,' put the Channel between him and England, and sought an asylum in France.

When St. John was a boy of three-and-twenty, he confided to Sir William Trumbull that he was ambitious of pushing himself into business, because he had good grounds—*res angusta domi*—to desire

an employment. ' It would vex a man,' said he, ' to
learn with pain and trouble how to serve his country,
and yet not be able to do it, and this, I fear, is the case
among those few that are honest in public station.
Like a painter of whom I have read somewhere that
went into a battle and lost both his arms, he came back
with lively images of all he had seen, but without the
power of putting them on canvas.' That which St.
John had suggested fourteen years ago had, by a cruel
irony of fate, come true. Not only had he learned
with pain and trouble how to serve his country ; he
had served her with zeal in time of war, he had brought
peace to her with the rare skill and energy which were
his. And he was able to serve her no longer.

An attainted man, he suffered for his share in the
Peace of Utrecht and for that share alone. The Whigs
saw too good a chance to lose of ridding themselves for
ever of the wisest and most eloquent of the Tories, and
while they profited exceedingly by the period of calm
and tranquillity which he had given to England, they
made no scruple of ruining him who had given it.
Political history shows no starker tragedy, no more
malign injustice. Bolingbroke had always maintained a lofty sense of duty. ' Neither Montaigne in
writing his essays,' he wrote, ' nor Descartes in building
new worlds knew, nor Newton in discovering and
establishing true the laws of nature on a sublime
geometry felt more intellectual joys that he feels who
is a real patriot, who bends all the force of his understanding and directs all his thoughts and actions to the
good of his country.'

From these intellectual joys he was henceforth debarred. He was like the painter of whom he wrote in his youth, the painter who had lost both his arms. He was like an actor deprived of a stage, a singer robbed of his voice, a soldier maimed of his right hand. The mere opportunity of exercising his craft was taken from him, and he was no more than thirty-seven, the age at which many men are only beginning their career. There he was, a young man, with his gifts sacrificed to the ambition of a rival. Never again might his eloquence astonish or convince his peers. Never again might he fight with his voice against the men who he believed were bringing this country to ruin. He was, moreover, of those who love the dust more than the palm. He had 'from nature a mind better pleased with the struggle than the victory.' As he pitied those who were prevented from serving their country by tyranny, so he despised the others who renounced that service for the pleasures of life or of the chase. And though he knew that he deserved pity, his pride resented it that any one should take compassion on him. He bore his loss with the courage bred of arrogance. Bitterly as he felt his own failure and the triumph of Walpole, he refused to repine or complain. 'I am still the same proscribed man,' he wrote to Windham, 'surrounded with difficulties, exposed to mystifications, and unable to take any share in the public service. . . . My part is over, and he who remains on the stage after his part is over deserves to be hissed off.' Bolingbroke was not hissed off : he went.

BOLINGBROKE

II

HE arrived in Paris in July 1715. The town was agog with plot and counterplot. A disorderly multitude was at work, and every one was doing what seemed right in his own eyes. 'Care and hope,' said Bolingbroke, 'sat on every busy Irish face,' and the hope without reason eclipsed the care. Though his false reception as an emissary to the Pretender from the Tories irked him so bitterly that he sought refuge in Dauphiné, to remove the reproach of living near the Court of France, gradually he was drawn within the net, and played his part in the tortuous policy and abject failure of the Jacobites. 'The smart of the attainder,' said he, 'tingled in every vein'; he believed, rightly enough, that his party was oppressed, and needed his help; and his misery was increased by the disillusionment which followed his first conversation with the Pretender. 'He talked like a man,' said Bolingbroke, 'who expected every moment to set out for England or Scotland, but who did not very well know for which.' The sanguine expectation, in which the Pretender and his friends lived, was enough to destroy the surest enterprise. The Jacobite

Ministry was a mob of babblers, male and female, to whom nothing was sacred or secret. Fanny Ogle-thorpe had a place in it, and Olive Trant, and the notorious Abbé de Tessieu, who 'stooped,' said Bolingbroke, 'to the lure of a Cardinal's hat.' They chattered and conspired in a hidden villa of the Bois de Boulogne, whither Bolingbroke was asked to find his way, furtively and uselessly. Into such company was fallen, for his sins, the proud Secretary of State. When the inevitable ruin came, the Jacobites threw the blame upon Bolingbroke, and hinted amiably that he had diverted a great sum of the Pretender's money to his own uses ! When all was finished, Lord Stair was given full power to treat with the fallen Minister, to enter into a treaty to reverse his attainder, and to stipulate upon what terms this act of grace should be granted. Bolingbroke dismissed all thought of a treaty. ' If the court,' said he, ' believed these pro-fessions to be sincere, a treaty with me was unnecessary for them ; and if they did not believe them so, a treaty with them was dangerous for me.'

He settled him down to bear his banishment with what spirit he might. And as though to fortify his mind against disaster, he composed (in 1716) his *Reflections upon Exile*. Following Montaigne, he let another speak for him, and he made his plaint out of the spoils of other men. Montaigne bade Plutarch interpret his thoughts, and Bolingbroke called in Seneca to bring him comfort. Neither the French-man nor the Englishman may be charged with insincerity for this dependence. They found in the ancients the sentiments which belonged to them, and held it no shame to translate rather than to invent. The reflections are marked by the courage we should expect of their author. Here is no pathetic discourse. Bolingbroke writes as one who 'never trusted to Fortune even while she seemed to be at peace with him.' Like Seneca, he made light of exile. He regarded it as a life of simplicity and diminished care. Where his soul was, there was he at home. In brief, he was able to find consolation in the commonplaces of the philosophers, and yet, despite his brave resolution, he resembles now and again a man who blows a little noisily on his fingers to keep them warm.

Having rejected the treaty which Lord Stair would have made with him, he was henceforth an outlaw. Some privileges were restored to him. In 1723 he was pardoned, and two years afterwards was graciously permitted to inherit and acquire real estate. But Walpole was far too harsh a partisan ever to permit the man whom he feared to sit in parliament again. The career, then, which Bolingbroke had chosen himself was at an end and never to be revived. He could fight his enemies with a tireless energy in *The Craftsman* and other journals ; he could rely upon the loyal aid of Windham and Pulteney, the ' Patriots '; there was no place where the eloquence which was wont to subdue the Senate could be heard again. If he might no longer take his place in the battlefield, he might at least survey the combat from afar, and give good counsel to those for whose cause he would willingly have drawn the sword.

Henceforth he gave himself up to a country life and the Muses. He had found a serene happiness in his second marriage with Mme. de Villette, and he was fortunate in his friendships. To Swift and Pope, to Gay and Arbuthnot he remained bound in the ties of affection unto the end of his life or theirs. The letters which these wise men exchanged attest their loyalty one to another. They took a just pride both in the manner and the sentiment of their correspondence. They could not help addressing one another with a certain pomp and circumstance. They were the true sons of their age, who preferred to be found on parade, even in their comradeship. 'I seek no epistolary fame,' wrote Bolingbroke to Swift in a moment of self-deception, 'but am a good deal pleased to think that it will be known hereafter that you and I lived in the most friendly intimacy together.' Surely it is known, and the names of Swift and Bolingbroke will be linked together unto the end of time.

Thus sustained by friendship Bolingbroke spent his years in study and seclusion. He had learned, he told Swift, to be unfortunate without being unhappy. He lived out of the world, as he did not blush to own, and out of the fashion. A bitter experience had taught him that he could not serve the present age, and, said he, 'I have a mind to write for the next age.' So, whether in Touraine or at Dawley, he read and wrote and played the farmer. His farming was less serious, no

doubt, than his reading and his writing, but it con-
formed to the fashion of the time, and was pursued
with all the elegance of pastoral poetry.   It was not
for him to return to nature ; he loved artifice even in
his country life ; and the frugality, of which he sometimes boasted, was, as his censor, Swift, well knew, but
a pleasant jest. 'Now his Lordship,' once wrote
Pope to Swift from Dawley, 'is run after his cart, I
have a moment left to myself to tell you that I over-
heard him yesterday agree with a painter for £200 to
paint his country hall with rakes, spades, prongs, etc.,
and other ornaments, merely to countenance his
calling the place a farm.'

His life of study needed no countenance.   In a
letter to Lord Bathurst he sketched the happiness
of his own retirement.   Truly he made the best
of his forced exclusion from public affairs. 'While
we remain in the world,' said he, 'we are all
fettered down more or less to one common level,
and have neither all the leisure nor all the means
and advantages to soar above it, which we may procure for ourselves by breaking these fetters in retreat.'
None saw more clearly than he that the desire of
knowledge and the love of study must have grown up
with us, and he could take some comfort in the thought
that not even his youthful pleasures had interfered
with his natural industry and application. 'To set
about acquiring the habits of meditation and study late
in life,' he wrote, 'is like getting into a go-cart with a
grey beard, or learning to walk when we have lost the

use of our legs. In general the foundations of a happy old age must be laid in youth : and in particular he who has not cultivated his reason young will be utterly unable to improve it old.' Nor did he echo the common complaints about the shortness of life and the lack of time. These he held to be the grumblings of the vulgar. We had ample leisure, thought he, for the business and the pleasure of life and something over. 'When we have secured the necessaries '— such was his opinion—'there may be time to amuse ourselves with the superfluities, and even with the trifles of life. *Dulce est desipere,* said Horace : *Vive la Bagatelle,* says Swift. I oppose neither ; not the Epicurean, much less the Christian Philosopher ; but I insist that a principal part of these amusements is the amusement of study and reflection, of reading and conversation. You know what conversation I mean ; for we lose the advantage of our nature and constitution, if we suffer the mind to come, as it were, to a stand.' Thus having assured himself leisure, he knew that one necessary thing remained—to keep his mind upon the straight path of study. ' I am sensible,' he confessed, ' more sensible than any enemy I have of my natural disadvantages : but I have begun and I will persist, for he who jogs forward on a battered horse in the right way, may get to the end of his journey, which he cannot do who gallops the fleetest courser of Newmarket out of it.'

And for him the right way lay towards study and expression. He had been a student ever since he

visited France and Italy on his grand tour.   For
expression too he had a natural aptitude.   He was
born with a gift for writing, and he had sedulously
cultivated his gift.   His style is the style of tongue
appealing to ear.   His works are written oratory.
Keeping in mind the precepts of eloquence, he shows
himself unafraid of long sentences.   And his long
sentences are never out of hand.   His words are held
together by so firm a thread of meaning, and argument,
and sound, that they never fall apart or are dispersed.
Chesterfield, by no means the worst critic of his time,
thought Bolingbroke's style superior to anybody's.
Until he read *The Patriot King*, he confesses that he
did not know the extent and powers of the English
language, and vainly did he recommend the author to
his son for imitation.

Bolingbroke's reading was wide and deep.   He had
explored with zeal and understanding the ancients
as well as the moderns.   And being a country gentleman of leisure and studious habits, he thought it
his duty to become a philosopher and a theologian.
He made of metaphysics a stick wherewith to beat
the metaphysicians.   A stern Erastian in politics, an
ardent lover of the State Church, he proclaimed himself a Deist on paper, and won the undying hate of the
orthodox.   He had a firm faith in natural religion,
and he set reason on a lofty throne.   For whatever
was mystical he had a profound contempt, and he
charged the atheist and divine with being in a con-
spiracy together.   To Pope he was an inspiration, and

he supplied the prose which Pope translated into the poetry of the *Essay on Man*. With just cause he took a legitimate pride in the instruction which he had given to his friend, and the friend rewarded him by a handsome dedication. 'Let me refer you to our friend Pope,' he writes to Lord Bathurst. 'He says I made a philosopher of him : I am sure he has contributed very much, and I thank him for it, to the making a hermit of me.'

While the hermit took pleasure in theological speculation, he knew that the true bent of his mind was towards history and political philosophy. History he studied in the wise, easy manner of his age. Centuries were the units of his observation, not years, and in painting the past as he saw it, he employed a large brush and vivid colours. In his eyes, truly, history was no mere science to be pursued for its own sake. He cared little for accuracy, and he had an unjust contempt for the archæologist. He would rather take Darius, whom Alexander conquered, for the son of Hystaspes, than sacrifice half his life to collect the learned lumber that fills the head of the antiquary. He regarded history as a training in private and public virtue. He would learn from the past how to interpret and conduct the affairs of the present. And so, quoting Dionysius of Halicarnassus, he defined history as philosophy teaching by examples. He looked to it always for profitable instruction. His view of it was not unlike Montaigne's, for whom Amyot's Plutarch was a touchstone of morals as well

as a breviary, and who tested his own life and the life
of his time by the example of Plutarch's heroes.   As
he says himself, he did not care what name Achilles
bore when he lived among the maids, nor did he
inquire what songs the sirens sang — problems
which Sir Thomas Browne thought not insoluble.

The mistress of human life, as he called history, had
not any concern with these toys of curiosity, which
were incapable of improving us in wisdom and virtue.
What he sought was, to repeat his own phrase, philosophy teaching by examples.   The need of this
philosophy was always apparent to him.   'Such is
the imperfection of human understanding,' said he,
'such the frail temper of our minds, that abstract or
general propositions, though ever so true, appear
obscure or doubtful to us very often, till they are
explained by examples.'   As in philosophy mysticism
was beyond the reach of his hard, practical intelligence,
so in history one concrete example was more to his
purpose than a dozen prudent maxims.   Moreover,
examples have this advantage, that they appeal to our
passions as well as to our understandings.   Nevertheless in his instant demand for fair examples he did not
underrate the value of experience, for which he thought
history was a necessary preparation.   History should
precede experience, indeed, and not supplant it.   And
since to converse with historians is to keep good company, it follows that it is of great profit to prepare
ourselves by this conversation for that of the world,
and to receive our first impressions, to acquire our first

habits, in a scene where images of virtue and vice are continually represented to us in the shapes that properly belong to them.

Thus in Bolingbroke's eyes history was a school of moral and worldly instruction, and it has this advantage over the school of experience, that its lessons are presented to us in a complete form. We do not always live to see the consequences of our own actions. History shows us causes, as in fact they are laid, with their immediate effects, and enables us to guess at future events. And in these words Bolingbroke concludes his panegyric upon history : ' since the ages of prophecy, as of miracles, are past, we must content ourselves to guess at what will be, by what has been : we have no other means in our power, and history furnishes us with these.' How many men of our time have been at the pains to put history to this valuable use ?

When Bolingbroke sate himself down to instruct his country in the arts of good government, his mind was richly stored with the examples of the past. The achievements in statecraft of the Greeks and Romans were ever before him. His admiration of our own Elizabeth is loudly expressed. But the most of his sermons are preached to a more modern text. For him the great landmark of history is the Revolution of 1688, the results of which, for all his coquetry with the Jacobites, he accepted without reserve. He had an unbounded admiration for the British Constitution, because it had nothing to do with what he called a simple form of government, and by that he meant a form of government which lodged the supreme power, absolutely and without control, either in a single person, or in particular persons of the community, or in the whole body of the people. Of this form the two worst, he thought, were absolute monarchy, which is tyranny, and absolute democracy, which is tyranny and anarchy both. Of absolute monarchy, history, if not his own experience, furnished him with many specimens. To him absolute democracy can have been a dream and no more. It is a dismal reality for us. After many years of a well-balanced government, we have resorted to the simplest form yet known to the world—an absolute democracy in which the minority pays the taxes, and the majority, consisting of manual workers, alone has any real power or strength. In his happier time Bolingbroke could still applaud the English Constitution, even though he denounced those who used it merely for their own ends. ' If liberty be that delicious fruit,' he wrote in his *Dissertation upon Parties*, ' on which the British nation has fed for so many ages, the British Constitution is the tree that bears this fruit, and will continue to bear it as long as we are careful to fence it in, and trench it round against the beasts of the field, and the insects of the earth.' We have neither fenced it in nor trenched it round, and to-day the beasts of the field and the insects of the earth may devour it without let or hindrance.

Bolingbroke knew well that it was its tripartite

character which gave the English Constitution its
strength and beauty. ' It is this mixture of monar-
chical, aristocratical, and democratical power,' said he,
' blended together in one system and by these three
estates balancing one another, that our free constitution of government hath been preserved so long, or
hath been brought back, after having suffered violation,
to its original principles.' With each step of its
progress he was content. The throne, as time had
fashioned it, was beyond the reach of his criticism.
' The King of Britain,' he wrote, ' is now strictly and
properly what kings should always be, a member, but
a supreme member, or the head, of a political body :
part of one individual and specific whole, in every
respect, distinct from it or independent of it in name :
he can move no longer in another orbit from his people,
and like some superior planet, repel, influence, and
direct their motions by his own. . . . The settle-
ments, by virtue of which he governs, are plainly
original contracts. His institution is plainly con-
ditional, and he may perfect his right to allegiance, as
undeniably and as effectually as the subject may perfect
his right to protection.' In his view of kingship, then,
Bolingbroke did not differ much from the Whigs, and
justified his opinion that King James must have died
on the throne if the Tories had not concurred to place
the Prince of Orange there in his stead.

As he applauded loudly and candidly the position
and the functions of the King, so he appreciated at
their true worth the duty and danger of parliaments.

c

'Parliaments,' said he, 'are the true guardians of liberty. For this principally they are instituted, and this is the principal article of that great and noble trust, which the collective body of the people repose in the representative. But no slavery can be so effectively brought and fixed upon us as parliamentary slavery. By the corruption of parliament we return into that state to deliver or secure us from which parliaments were instituted. . . . That noble fabric, which was able to resist so many races of giants, may be demolished by a race of pygmies. The integrity of parliament is a sort of palladium, a tutelary goddess, who protects our state. When she is once removed, we may become the prey of any enemies.'

Bolingbroke surveyed the working of the British Constitution, and saw that parliament was corrupt and the country enslaved. He brushed aside the excuses of Walpole and his friends with bitter contempt. 'These men are ready to tell us,' said he, 'that corruption serves to oil the wheels of government, and to render the administration more smooth and easy, and that it can never be of dangerous consequence under the present father of the country. Absurd and wicked triflers!' So much he saw. His political imagination could not picture to him a state in which the votes of the whole people are bought by doles and promises, and in which every citizen may claim his price, if he will. Even as he saw it, the state of things was ugly enough. 'When a people crouch, like camels to be loaded, the next at hand, no matter who,

mounts them, and they soon feel the whip and spear
of their tyrant; for a tyrant, whether prince or
minister, resembles the devil in many respects,
particularly in this : he is often both the tempter and
the tormentor. He makes the criminal and he
punishes the crime.'

What, then, should be done to give the constitution
free play and to save the nation from tyranny ?
Bolingbroke urged the abolition of faction, which has
no regard to national interests. The peace and
prosperity of a nation, he thought, depended upon
uniting as far as possible the heads, hearts, and hands
of the whole people, and upon improving, not debauch-
ing, its morals. Though the sentiment may seem a
commonplace, it was then and is still a piece of the
wildest idealism. And it was the politicians alone
who were determined to make a god of corruption.
' It is time,' said Bolingbroke, ' that all who desire to
be esteemed good men and to procure the peace, the
strength, and the glory of their country, should join
their efforts to heal our national divisions, and to change
the narrow spirit of party into a diffusive spirit of
public benevolence.' To make this change one thing
was necessary—the formation of a country party.
And what was a country party ? ' A country party
must be authorised by the voice of the country. It
must be formed on principles of common interest. It
cannot be united and maintained on the particular
prejudices, any more than it can or ought to be
directed to the particular interests, of any set of men

whatsoever. A party thus constituted is improperly called a party ; it is the nation speaking and acting in the discourse and conduct of particular men.'

Had Bolingbroke been able to make his ideal a reality, England would have returned to the pristine happiness of the Garden of Eden. The party of his imagining, so wide in compass that it embraced all our citizens, so closely compact in union that it had but one thought, one hope, would have made short work of the class-favouritism, the corruption, the narrow personal ambition of the Whigs. Such a party never has been, never will be seen (I fear) in this world of frailty and self-seeking. Though Bolingbroke called it a coalition, it had nothing to do with those conspiracies which have borne the name, conspiracies not to unite the people, but to keep a few greedy ministers perpetually in office and to distribute such preferment as the Government disposes of among rich and obedient supporters. Yet Bolingbroke's dream was not dreamed wholly in vain. It was a momentary inspiration to a band of idealists in the nineteenth century, and (who knows ?) it may yet animate some among our own contemporaries to a larger, wiser policy of selflessness.

The first quality necessary for the abolishing of faction is patriotism, and in an *Essay on Patriotism* Bolingbroke has analysed with all his eloquence and skill the duty and character of a patriot. As I have said, he took a lofty view of statesmanship. He complained with Socrates that while no man undertakes

a trade, even the meanest, without training, every one
thinks himself sufficiently qualified for the hardest of
all trades—the trade of government. Now, the trade
of government, in his eyes, was as greatly ennobling
as it was difficult. He made a lively contrast between
the works and actions of great men with the works
and actions of cunning politicians. Great men, he
thought, might easily be detected. 'They observe
with distinction,' he wrote ; ' they advise with knowledge. They may indulge themselves in pleasure,
but as their industry is not employed about trifles, so
their amusements are not made the business of their
lives. If they retire from the world, their splendour
accompanies them, and enlightens even the obscurity
of their retreat. If they take a part in public life, the
effect is never indifferent. They either appear like
ministers of divine vengeance, or they are the guardian
angels of the country they inhabit.' If he is under
the suspicion of having cast himself for this *beau rôle*,
there is no doubt that in sketching his opposite he kept
his eye upon Walpole. 'We will suppose a man,'
thus he wrote, ' imprudent, rash, presumptuous, un-
gracious, insolent, and profligate in speculation as in
practice. He can bribe, but he cannot seduce : he
can buy, but he cannot gain : he can lie, but he
cannot deceive. From whence, then, has such a
man his strength ? From the general corruption
of the people, nursed up to a full maturity under his
administration ; from the venality of all orders and
all ranks of men, some of whom are so prostitute,

that they set themselves to sale and even prevent application.'

Thus Bolingbroke held that, until the millennium brought with it a united country, purged of faction, it was the patriot's duty to oppose, when he was not permitted to lead the government of his country. I think it was Bolingbroke who first reduced to form and order what was required of an opposition. He asked no less of it than he did of a government. ' They who affect to lead an opposition,' said he, ' must be equal at least to those whom they oppose ; I do not say in parts only, but in application and industry, and the fruits of both—information, knowledge, and a certain constant preparedness for all the events that may arise. Every administration is a system of conduct. Opposition should be a system of conduct likewise ; an opposite but not an independent system.' Never has the duty of an opposition been more clearly explained, and when we see it efficiently and wisely discharged we may reconcile ourselves to the dangers of partisan government.

So Bolingbroke passed from the patriot citizen to the patriot king, his treatise upon whom is still the best known of his works. He pictured his ideal monarch as influenced by no party in the state, as sincerely zealous for the welfare of all his subjects. He thought that a limited monarchy was the best of governments, and an hereditary monarchy the best of monarchies. He believed in the divine right of kings to govern well. ' A divine right to govern ill,' said he, ' is an absurdity : to assert it is blasphemy.' He held that the true end of all governments is the good of the people, for whose sake they are made, and without whose consent they could not have been made, that the king and the people take a sort of engagement with one another, the prince to govern well, and the people to honour and obey him. Between the king and the people in a free government there is not, there cannot be, any rivalry. A patriot king will make but one distinction between his rights and those of his people : he will look upon his to be a trust and theirs to be a property. At his coming, faction will disappear, and corruption will cease to be an expedient of government. As his opportunity will be great, great also must be his devotion. He must begin to govern as soon as he begins to reign, and take upon his willing shoulders the burden of responsibility. Knowing full well the end at which he aims himself, he will call to his administration such men as he can assure himself will serve in the same principles in which he intends to govern. A good prince—and good he must be if he be a patriot—will no more choose ill men than a wise prince will choose fools. In brief, says Bolingbroke, ' to espouse no party, but to govern like the common father of his people is so essential to the character of a patriot king, that he who does otherwise forfeits the title.'

He saw in the happy time that was to come the true image of a free people, governed by a patriot king—a patriarchal family, whose head and members

are united by one interest, and animated by one
spirit.   If only we attained to this blessing, he
believed that all the others would be added to us.
' In the place of civil fury,' said he in an eloquent
passage, ' concord will appear, brooding peace and
prosperity on the happy land ; a people unoppressed,
undisturbed, unalarmed ; busy to improve their private
property and the public stock ; fleets covering the
ocean, bringing home wealth by the returns of
industry, carrying assistance or terror abroad by the
direction of wisdom, and asserting triumphantly
the right and the honour of Great Britain, as far
as waters roll and as winds can waft them.'   Thus
he defined the aim of all his teaching ; thus he
expressed the one hope that was left him.   And he
desired life for nothing so much as to see a king of
Great Britain the most greatly beloved man in his
country, a patriot at the head of a united people.
Popular kings we have seen.   The spectacle of a
united people is denied us, as it was denied to
Bolingbroke.

Bolingbroke passed from middle life to age a proscribed man.   He alone of the King's subjects was
forbidden to take his share in the government of his
country ; to him alone was denied access to those
affairs whose management he had pondered more
deeply and wisely than any other among his contemporaries.   Always a proscribed man, he was long an exile.
When he retired to his ' old and decayed mansion in
Battersea,' to-day half ruin, half workshop, with

nothing left to attest its grandeur save the panels of his own favourite room, ' I go to my own country,' he wrote, ' as if I went in to a strange country, and shall inhabit my own house as if I lodged in an inn.' [1] His active career was over, over soon after it was begun. He was left without hope for himself, with undying hope for his country. Whoever seemed a patriot in his eyes, him would he fortify with encouragement and wise counsel. Pulteney and Windham might rely upon his aid and his support. To William Pitt, rising from the cornetcy of horse to the governance of England, he was a constant inspiration. Chesterfield, who saw him but a few days before his death, had never ceased to frequent and admire him. Thus, unconquered by misfortune, and indeed unconquerable, Bolingbroke faced age and disease and the end with an equal mind. ' I will swallow down the dregs of life,' said he, ' as quickly and as calmly as I can.' His wife's death in 1750 left him desolate and brave. As his years increased, the friends, whose amiable converse had meant a vast deal to him, preceded him to the grave. There was left to him only the fidelity of a sister, whose fate had been unhappier than his own.

When Bolingbroke died, in 1751, an inscription, composed by his own hand, was cut upon his monument, and it contains a deeper truth than is generally consistent with the lapidary style. ' Here lies Henry St. John,' thus it runs, ' in the reign of Queen Anne, Secretary of War, Secretary of State, and Viscount

[1] See *The Marchmont Papers*, quoted by Mr. Walter Sichel.

Bolingbroke. In the days of King George I. and King George II. something more and better.' Truly the author of *The Patriot King*, the wise political philosopher, deserves and has won a higher respect than the eloquent partisan who fought for a faction in the Queen's reign. If the privilege of open speech were denied him, he practised the art of prose with a skill and understanding which were beyond the scope of his contemporaries. If his influence waned, it was never totally extinguished, and, potent as it was in the days of Young England, it may even in these darker times recover its ancient power. It is true that he never witnessed the formation of that country party which should restore the fortunes of England. Yet he did not despair. 'We read in the Old Testament,' said he, 'of a city that might have escaped divine vengeance if five righteous men had been found in it. Let not our city perish for want of so small a number ; and if the generation that is going off could not furnish it, let the generation that is coming on furnish a greater.'

BUBB DODINGTON

'DULCE et decorum est pro patria mori,' says the poet. He might have added, with equal truth, that to live for the fatherland is neither sweet nor comely. They who live for the fatherland are wont also to live on the fatherland. 'Service is obligation, and obligation implies return,' says Bubb Dodington, summing up in these few candid words the purpose which has inspired politicians ever since popular government was invented. Dodington, indeed, faithfully respected the ancient tradition of his craft ; his example has been piously followed by those who came after him ; and if we would understand the strange processes by which the destinies of our country are controlled, we cannot do better than study the industrious, fruitless career of him who followed the trade of statesmanship for nearly half a century without losing sight of quarter-day, and who finally adopted for his own Rabelais' motto : *Et tout pour la trippe.*

George Bubb[1] was born in 1691, with five boroughs

[1] When Browning wrote a 'parleying' with him, Bubb Dodington was fading into forgetfulness. The 'parleying,' partially intelligible, ends on a couplet, which all can understand—

'folks see but one
Fool more, as well as knave, in Dodington.'

In *Patriot and Place-Hunter*, Mr. Lloyd Sanders gathered together all that ever need be known about this master of intrigue.

in his mouth.   His father, Jeremiah, said to have
been a Weymouth apothecary, was lucky enough to
marry Mary, the only sister of George Dodington, a
Dorsetshire squire.   The good fortune of the father
descended tenfold to the son.   He was brought up as
became his uncle's heir, from Winchester went to
Exeter College, Oxford, where he won an easy reputation as a poet, was returned to Parliament by George
Dodington's own borough of Winchelsea when he
was no more than twenty-three, and a year later set
out for Spain as Envoy Extraordinary, that he might
see the world and thus prepare for the ' statesmanship '
which was to be his trade.   Nor was his time wasted.
If he learned nothing else at Madrid, he learned,
in conflict with Alberoni, the ease and value of
political corruption, which solved differences of
opinion far more speedily than argument ever could
have done.

For George Bubb service abroad was but an interlude.   After two years' sojourn at Madrid he resumed
the duties of member for Winchelsea, and warmly
espoused the cause of Walpole.   In 1720 the death
of his uncle made him the master of a large fortune
and of the five boroughs, which conferred upon him,
during a long life, place and influence and power.
And the death of his uncle brought him something
more than a ready-made position in politics : it
ensured him a change of name.   Henceforth he was
to be known as Dodington, and the memory of Jeremiah, his offending father, would as far as possible

be wiped out. Alas ! the Bubb that was in him died hard. The satirists among his enemies—and his enemies were not few—did their best to perpetuate it, and as Bubb, Bubo, or even Bubington, was he known until the end.

When he emerged from the chrysalis of Bubb into the butterfly (or moth) that was Dodington, he was assuredly possessed of many advantages. Wealth was his in abundance, and the estate of Eastbury, where he spent £140,000 in finishing his uncle's house, gave him a dignity and importance which were felt far beyond the boundaries of his own county. However ill-chosen his friends may have been, he had a true gift of hospitality. He delighted to fill Eastbury, and afterwards La Trappe, his famous villa at Hammersmith, with guests and sycophants, and no slur was ever cast upon the quality of his Burgundy. His taste in decoration was opulent rather than refined. He had a natural love of marble pillars and columns of lapis-lazuli, of costly furniture and Greek statues. And yet even in his splendour a kind of tawdriness was always intervening, as though Bubb was still looking over the shoulder of Dodington. His own state-bed, for instance, a glory of Eastbury, was surrounded by a carpet embroidered in gold and silver, which betrayed its origin from old coats, waistcoats, and breeches, by the impregnable testimony of pockets, button-holes, and loops. The breeches, turned to the purpose of ornament, were typical of his character. 'See ! sportive Fate,' writes Pope :—

'to punish awkward pride
Bids Bubo build, and sends him such a guide:
A standing sermon, at each year's expense,
That never coxcomb reached magnificence.'

His wit was better than his taste. His reputation
for this, the rarest of all gifts, which envious time
does not preserve, is well founded upon the evidence of
his foes. Horace Walpole, who had no reason to
love him, admits that Lord Hervey and Dodington
' were the only two he ever knew who were always
aiming at wit, and generally found it,' and surely the
specimen, which he quotes—a translation of the motto
on the caps of the soldiers of the Hanoverians, *vestigia
nulla retrorsum*, 'they never mean to go back'—is
vastly to his credit. Unfortunately for his memory,
his diary is utterly devoid of the one quality in which
he excelled. He displays in it no glimmer of his wit,
and being a politician he had no hint of humour. It
is true that Pope dismisses him as 'a half-wit.' 'I
wonder not,' he writes to Swift, 'that Bubb paid you
no sort of civility while he was in Ireland. He is
too much of a half-wit to love a true-wit, and too
much half-honest to esteem any entire merit.' So
sincere was Pope in his hatred of Dodington, that he
shrank from his friendly approach. 'I hope, and I
think, he hates me too,' said he, 'and I will do my
best to make him. He is so insupportably insolent
in his civility to me when he meets me at one third
place, that I must affront him to be rid of it.' However, in Pope's despite, Dodington still stands among

the wits, and ambitious as he was to write verses himself, he took a simple delight in the society of poets.
He was constantly on the look-out for talent, and it
was part of his coxcomb's magnificence to play the
patron's part.   There was nothing he loved so much
as a dedication, and all were welcome at Eastbury who
would sing its owner's praise.   Sometimes his importunity met with rebuff, and one failure at least was
fortunate for him.   He solicited in vain the friendship
of Samuel Johnson, and thus escaped an encounter
which would not have flattered him.   Had the two
met in Boswell's presence, we should be the richer for
half-a-dozen pages.   But Dodington could never
have cajoled the Philosopher with the skill of John
Wilkes, and Johnson would have tolerated his coxcombry as little as he would have borne with his
inveterate Whiggishness.

If he missed Johnson, he attached to himself, even
in undying print, two such great men as Henry Fielding and James Thomson.   Truly Fielding was not
on oath when he wrote his poem, ' Of True Greatness,' and yet it cannot have been a happy memory
to him.   With a lavish hand he covered with flattery
the trafficker in boroughs.   Let us hope that the
genius of satire came to his aid when he penned
these lines :

> ' Some greatness in myself perhaps I view;
>   Not that I write, but that I write to you.'

This is bad enough, and the eulogy becomes grosser

as it is more precise. With yet greater effrontery
Fielding celebrates his patron's poems :

> 'Yourself th' unfashionable lyre have strung,
> Have own'd the Muses and their darling young.
> All court their favour when by all approved;
> E'en virtue, if in fashion, would be loved.
> You for their sakes with fashion dare engage,
> Mæcenas you in no Augustan age.'

And those lines were bound up in the same work
which contained a supreme masterpiece of irony—
'Jonathan Wild ! '

If some there were who doubted his pretension to
wit, all were agreed that he was a coxcomb. He lived
pompously and in the public eye. His clothes had the
same sort of magnificence as his houses. Wherever
he went he was pointed out with the finger rather
of ridicule than of respect. Chesterfield, who was
quicker than any of his contemporaries to distinguish
between the true and the false in life and manners,
gave him an eminence in coxcombry. 'With submission to my Lord Rochester,' he wrote, ' God made
Dodington the coxcomb he is ; mere human means
could not have brought it about. He is a coxcomb
superior to his parts, though his parts are superior to
almost anybody's. He is thoroughly convinced of the
beauty of his person, which cannot be worse than it is
without deformity.' As Walpole allows him wit, so
Chesterfield allows him parts, and then confesses that
' what it is difficult for him to do, he even overrates
his own parts.' In truth, he was no common cox-

comb. ' Common coxcombs,' says Chesterfield, ' hope
to impose upon others more than they impose upon
themselves ; Dodington is sincere, nay, moderate :
for he thinks still ten times better of himself than he
owns. Blest coxcomb ! '

The fine irony of this passage pictures us Dodington
as he was. Of what use were wit and parts, if they
were not protected from ridicule and contempt by
judgment and discretion ? And there was something
heroic in Dodington's accepting the rôle of coxcomb
put upon him by Providence. He triumphed over
the obstacles of mind and body. He was very fat.
Horace Walpole's brother, Ned, said he was ' grown
of less consequence and more weight,' and corpulence
and coxcombry do not agree. He was, moreover, of
those who, living in the world and pretending to
omniscience, understand nothing. Shelburne, a not
unkindly witness, describes him as ' a man who passed
his life with great men whom he did not know, and
in the midst of affairs which he never comprehended.'
And with him, says Shelburne, it was impossible to
formaliser. When Shelburne reminded him of a
piece of base conduct, Dodington replied : ' Well,
when did you know anybody get out of a great scrape
but by a great lye.' How could he fail to disarm
criticism, for the moment, by so open a confession ?

So it came about that he was one of those unfortunate people whom, in Hervey's phrase, ' it was the
fashion to abuse and ungenteel to be seen with.' In
spite of his ambition and pertinacity, he had a rare gift

D

of displeasing, a gift for which his boroughs alone were some sort of compensation. Though his attack upon politics was thus rendered more difficult, his spirit was undaunted. At any rate, he possessed one quality which always stands a politician in good stead,—he was wholly devoid of principles, prejudices, and convictions. He called himself a Whig, as the most of his contemporaries did, and he was an apt pupil of the Devil, the first of his kind. Had the Tories been strong enough, he would willingly have served them, and he made more than one attempt at a coalition. Backed by no principles, harbouring no opinions, he could be loyal neither to himself nor to the associates whom he could not honestly call friends. Hanbury-Williams hit him off in a few lines :

> ' To no one party, no one man,
>   Not to his ownself tight,
>   For what he voted for at noon,
>   He rail'd against at night.'

Nevertheless there remained the boroughs :

> ' One half of Winchelsea is mine,
>   And so's Bridgewater too ;
>   Poole, as you know, my wash-pot is,
>   O'er Wells I cast my shoe.'

It was natural, then, that at the outset he should follow the fortunes of Walpole. He saw that Minister safely entrenched in office, as he thought, for the term of his natural life, and the hope of profit followed his inclination. He heaped Walpole with flatteries in

exchange for honours and emoluments. He was made
a Lord of the Treasury and Clerk of the Pells in
Ireland, a pleasant sinecure which he kept until the
end of his life. It is characteristic of him that on one
of his rare visits to the country which gave him an
income he posed as a patriot, and in the true spirit of
the coxcomb arrayed himself in a suit made of Irish
material. Swift was quick with the retort that ' the
Irish Parliament made him a present of seven or eight
hundred a year for laying out forty or fifty shillings
on Irish stuff.' Not content with supporting Walpole, by a stroke of the ill-fortune which never
deserted him, in 1726 he composed a poem in the
Minister's honour, and set his devotion irrevocably
upon paper. A year later he had ratted, and one
unfortunate line—' in power a servant, out of power
a fiend,'—clung to him through all his life. Even if
the world had been willing to forget it, Pope would
not let it fall into oblivion, and at each new piece of
treachery Dodington was reminded of it.

Dodington's obsequiousness to Walpole lasted until
the death of George I., when he prematurely transferred his flattery, his devotion, and his boroughs to
Sir Spencer Compton, whom all the world marked
down as Walpole's successor. Leicester House, which
once seemed like a desert, was packed from morning
to night, ' like the 'Change at noon,' said an observer.
' But Sir Robert Walpole,' as Hervey tells us, ' walked
through those rooms as if they had been still empty ;
his presence, which used to make a crowd wherever

he appeared, now emptied every corner he turned to, and the same people who were officiously a week ago clearing the way to flatter his prosperity, were now getting out of it to avoid sharing his disgrace.' In politics it is ever the same—'farewell goes out sighing'; and Dodington was among the first to smile a welcome to Sir Spencer Compton. As usual, he overplayed his part. He showed himself base where he hoped to be cunning; and when Walpole returned instantly to the councils of the new King, after Sir Spencer's pitiful failure, Dodington was driven into opposition, and became the more bitterly rancorous because he knew that he was unforgiven.

If he could no longer assail Walpole with his flattery, he soon found another and, as he thought, a more profitable object of worship. The King's son, Frederick, Prince of Wales, soon followed his father to England, and in accord with a settled practice set up a rival court of his own. Dodington was among the first to bow the knee to the new prince, and was presently rewarded by being appointed adviser and first Minister. The letter, in which he announced his good intentions and sketched his simple hopes for the future, is characteristic of its author. ' I have set my whole heart,' wrote Dodington, ' on your happiness, but I place it in your glory, and this last in the welfare of our country. To see that life and gaiety, which makes you the delight of all that are near you, corrected by a severe probity and rigid honour, makes me everyday bless my good fortune and your partiality

to me ; but when I consider the happiness of millions
one day flowing from you, as the effect of that probity
and honour, I am thoroughly charmed with the
prospect, and am proud to own that your good opinion
does give one a pleasure that the friendship of a private
man could not give.'

The sincerity of the last sentence is at least unquestioned. The friendship of any man was as
nothing in Dodington's eyes, unless it could bring
him wealth and preferment. And he cared not a
jot how thickly he plastered his victims with vain
eulogy, if only he might use them for his own purpose.
To the Prince the gabble about glory and probity and
honour was probably unintelligible. He looked upon
Dodington with a sternly practical eye. He was not
at the pains to spell his name correctly, and in his
illiterate letters addressed him as Dorrington. He
found him and his wealth useful, and thought it a
clear proof of his folly that one day he was able, in
Shelburne's phrase, to ' touch him ' for £5000. Thus
for a while the ill-balanced friendship lasted. The
Prince and his satellite were neighbours as well as
friends, and Dodington had received the last gratifica-
tion of a key, which should admit him, when he would,
to Carlton House. The quarrel came soon, as it was
bound to come, since not even the Prince could have
confidence in the man who had already turned
against one benefactor, and interested conspirators
intensified the distrust. Nor was the discarded
favourite permitted to go quietly away. His fall was

duly advertised by the shrubs which were planted between his house and the Prince's garden, and by the changed locks of Carlton House.

No resource, then, was left for Dodington save to crawl back in all humility to Walpole. He was received with severity, and went obediently to heel. 'As to what you said,' Walpole told Hervey in 1735, 'about my enemies being great with impunity, I have told Dodington this very morning that I will no longer bear his shuffling, fast-and-loose conduct, and will rather risk the entering into the next session of Parliament with a majority only of forty or fifty than go on in this way. I desired, therefore, we might understand one another, and he has, with the greatest submission, promised everything I could require with regard to his future good behaviour.' Walpole's righteous insolence, which might have angered a better man, left Dodington unscathed. He merely pocketed his pride and doubled his resentment, and while he served Walpole openly, he lost no opportunity of fighting against him in secret. He showed great skill and pertinacity in organising oppositions, and it was not his fault that none of them succeeded. He acted for a while as the Duke of Argyll's spaniel, and when, in 1742, Walpole fell from power he was loudest in his insults to the ruined Minister. Sir Robert was content to dismiss 'Mr. Dodington, who had called his administration infamous, as a person of great self-mortification, who, for sixteen years, had condescended to bear part of the odium.'

So he sank in the public esteem, and in spite of his boroughs was compelled always to be in the minority, because no majority would accept him. At the first report of Culloden, says Horace Walpole, he 'came out with an illumination ; so pretty, that I believe he had it by him, ready for *any* occasion.' A few years later he is pictured as 'so reduced as to be relapsing into virtue.' And then in 1749, by a supreme stroke of luck, the Prince of Wales called him to his councils again. Once more he became one of the band of conspirators at Carlton House, who framed their mimic cabinets and dreamed of what they would do when the King died. Dodington was triumphant, and more frankly obsequious than ever. At last he had won the position and the influence which he had yearned for, and he was determined not to lose them. So proud was he of his place, so highly flattered by the honour done him, that he sat him down to compose a Diary, which is a document of surpassing value, and which displays in his true and lasting colours the complete politician. Lord Charlemont described it as 'the statesman's cabinet unlocked,' and the description is precisely accurate, if we put 'politician' for 'statesman.'

How the Diary came to be published is no less interesting than its cynical contents. Dodington's papers passed through the hands of Thomas Wyndham, who died in 1777, to Henry Penruddocke Wyndham, with a request 'not to print or publish any of them, but those that are proper to make publick, and such only as may, in some degree, do honour to his memory.'

Now, Henry Penruddocke Wyndham was a gentleman who lacked neither ingenuity nor candour. He admits at once that Dodington's conduct is proved by the Diary to ' have been wholly directed by the base motives of avarice, vanity, and selfishness.' How, then, should its publication do honour to Dodington's memory ? It depends wholly upon the meaning which we attach to Dodington's sense of honour. The editor makes no concealment of his own opinion, and he asks himself the question : ' How could I, with such sentiments of the Diary, venture to publish it, consistent with the clauses in the will ? ' He concludes from the care with which the Diary is copied out, that Dodington designed it for publication, and further meant it as an apology for his political conduct. In other words, he assumed that Dodington himself saw nothing dishonourable in his Diary, and though he did not agree with Dodington's estimate of the work, he felt bound to sacrifice his own judgment. ' The prejudices, perhaps, of education,' says he ingenuously, ' have instilled in my mind ideas of honour very different from those of his Lordship, which

> " putavi
> Stultus ego huic nostræ similes." '

It is an ingenious defence, which we may accept or not as we please, and Wyndham does not strengthen it by pretending that the Diary may inculcate a useful lesson ; that, in fact, ' the country gentlemen, in particular, may learn from it, that they have as much to dread from those who are in pursuit of power as from those in actual possession of it ; from those who are, hopefully, working in the cold climate of disappointment as from those who are luxuriously basking in the sunshine of enjoyment.' That the career of Dodington is an awful warning is true enough. It is true also that the warning has not been of the slightest service in purifying the morals of politicians. And though, when he printed the Diary, Henry Penruddocke Wyndham gave us a document of great value, it cannot be said that he did honour to his victim's memory.

In Dodington's Diary, as I have said, we see the complete politician displayed, with all his cunning, all his immorality, all his indifference. If any of the egoists who have since misgoverned the country had had the candour to expose their method and ambition, they would have used the same terms as served the ingenious Dodington. They have not the candour, and, so far as we know, none of them has set down upon paper a faithful record of his misdeeds. And here is Dodington as our guide, and what he did we may be sure many of his successors have done, if with less than his energy and resolution, with the best gifts they could summon to the task. Never once, then, did a thought of his country or a scruple of conscience disturb him. He knew only one aim, the advancement of Dodington, and one means, the discomfiture of Dodington's rivals. He was always talking of action, and he dealt in nothing but speech. As far as touched him, the government of the country was carried on by interminable arguments, held with those in whose hands lay the distribution of offices. It mattered not a jot what this man or that did when he got into office, it mattered a vast deal who got into office. The complete politician, then as now, was handicapped by no principles, no opinions, no prejudices. Dodington had as little humour as honour—humour is a quality fatal to politicians—and he saw nothing ridiculous in his shiftings and turnings, in his constant eavesdropping at the backstairs. The more secrets he knew the better for him, as he might turn them against his friends, if he were encumbered with such things, and make up in blackmail what he wanted in sagacity. When he was out for the hundred and fiftieth time the world laughed at him, and laughed especially at the gravity of his demeanour. So well did he play his losing game that at last nobody would be led by him, and yet, like the true artist that he was, he still followed his dreary craft for its own sake, though he must have known that nothing short of earthquakes and the deaths of kings could advance him.

He makes no pretence of taking an interest in the affairs of Great Britain. He was living and plotting through those great years in which the elder Pitt was establishing the British Empire all the world over, and the triumph of England did not for an hour disturb his sedulous intrigue. He does not mention Plassey or Quebec. If the names of Clive and Wolfe were ever borne to his ears, they were speedily forgotten. He was far too busy arguing with Ministers about his past services to show any interest in the victories of our British arms. He thought his duty accomplished when he had done his best to exclude Pitt from the management of affairs. If he had had his way we should have muddled through to hopeless disaster under the auspices of Newcastle, and Dodington would have thought the world well lost if only the ruins had struck him the proud Treasurer of the Navy. At any rate, he was furious when Pitt was given his golden opportunity, and not a crumb of comfort was thrown to him. Nothing shows his true character more clearly than his comment upon Pitt's happy accession to power. 'Thus ended this attempt,' he writes in his Diary, 'to deliver the King from hands he did not like.' It mattered not to the politician that those hands presently saved England.

His Diary is one of those documents which can never disappoint us. He discloses all that he said and thought with a candour which, as I have said, no other politician has equalled. From the very beginning of his second period of service under the Prince, Dodington settled down comfortably to that which he loved best—a life of cunning. If there were nobody to plot against, he would plot against himself rather than be idle. Happily for him, his enemies gave him plenty to do. When the Prince—in 1749—offered him 'the full return of his favour,' he was overjoyed. It is true, that for the moment he held office under Pelham, to whom he was pledged. As he knew no loyalty, so he speedily invented an excuse. ' I saw the country in so dangerous a condition,' he told Pelham, ' and found myself incapable to contribute to its relief and so unwelcome to attempt it, that I thought it misbecame me to receive great emoluments from a country whose service I could not, and if I could I should not, be suffered to promote.' The ingenuity of the excuse is admirable, and Dodington went down to Kew, proudly conscious of an act of high unselfishness. If he had renounced office, he had renounced it willingly, and the kindness of the Prince, who ' often admitted him to the honour of supping with him,' was sufficient reward.

The Prince marched boldly from words to deeds, and offered Dodington £2000 a year. The offer was not serious. The Prince was far more likely to ' touch ' his adviser than to pay him. But Dodington was always a stickler for form, and he humbly desired to stand upon the establishment without any salary, with the sole condition that he should take what the Prince designed for him when he should be King. The Prince, not a whit below Dodington as a comedian, solemnly assured him that, while it well became him to make the offer of voluntary service, it did not become him to accept it. And then they fell to bargaining. In truth, their favourite pastime was to cut up the skin before the bear was killed ! As soon as the King died, Dodington was to have a peerage, with the management of the House of Lords, and the seals of Secretary of State for the Southern Province. So

splendid was the prospect that he cared not a jot
whether he was paid his salary or not. He beguiled
the time spent at Kew pleasantly enough in devising
comfortable plans for himself and his friends, and in
praying that the King might be speedily removed to
a still more exalted sphere.

His good fortune did not escape envy. Enemies
sprang up in the very household of the Prince himself.
A rancorous pamphlet charged him—the blameless
Dodington—with intruding into the family to create
differences. His righteous indignation was unbounded. When he was urged to come to an explanation with the Prince, his air of startled innocence
suggested that he had never inspired a pamphlet in his
life, that he knew nothing about the act of undermining
a colleague. He cajoled, he importuned, he plotted
with Lord Middlesex or with any other who would
listen to him, he pleaded his own unworthiness.
'Every one had their faults,' he said; 'I might be
vain, I might be high, and yet mean very well, and be
made very useful.' There speaks the true Dodington,
who, in what he called 'transacting business,' was
indefatigable. He was ready to spend days, even
weeks, in talk, and if he did not convince his interlocutors, he must surely have bored them. How long
the Prince's patience would have endured the garrulity
of his humble servitor we do not know, for the argument was abruptly brought to a sudden end by the
Prince's death.

Thus, in a moment, Dodington's vision of peerages,

ribbons, and secretaryships of state vanished into thin air, and he was left friendless and alone. That he might serve the Prince, he had angered the King and deserted Pelham. He was neither dismayed nor abashed. He composed a funeral oration upon his master and himself, which Horace Walpole called *Bubb de tristibus*, and which he certainly did not intend should bloom and wither in obscurity. 'We have lost the delight and ornament of the age he lived in,' thus he wrote of the Prince, with whom he had been eagerly anticipating his father's death ; . . . 'we have lost the refuge of private distress, the balm of the afflicted heart, the shelter of the miserable against the fury of private calamity ; the arts, the graces, the anguish, the misfortunes of society have lost their patron and their remedy. I have lost my protector, my companion, my friend that loved me, that condescended to hear, to communicate, to share in all the pleasures and pains of the human heart, where the social affections and emotions of the mind only presided, without regard to the infinite disproportion of our rank and condition.' With much more to the same purport. And having disburdened his soul, he looked about him for a fresh patron, a fresh occasion of intrigue.

His task was not easy. So far he had never been faithful to the trust reposed in him. He had insulted Walpole, he had insulted Pelham, he had sided with the Prince against his father. At the very moment of the Prince's death he had been busy with a project which taxed to the full even his ingenuity. This was nothing less than a union between the independent Whigs and the Tories. The new Party, sketched by Dodington's sanguine mind, was to 'renounce all tincture of Jacobitism, and offer short but constitutional and revolutional principles.' Only a true politician could invent such principles as those —principles which were at once 'constitutional and revolutional'; and Dodington must have smiled with an inward satisfaction as he wrote the words. He thought, moreover, that 'there were good grounds to hope for a happy issue.' And then the Prince died. What could Dodington do but exclaim : 'Father of mercy, Thy hand, that wounds, alone can save !'

It will be seen that his hope—to unite the incompatibles, to abolish principles at a stroke—is the hope which has inspired the most of politicians who have lived and plotted since the time of Dodington. If only constitutional meant the same thing as revolutional, there would be no more strife, and the best and wisest of Prime Ministers, whoever he be, might be tenant for life of his high office. Of course, Dodington's plot of a new Party failed, as such plots always fail, and he had done nothing more than make a new crop of enemies. Neither his spirit nor his resource deserted him. He swore eternal fidelity to the widowed Princess, and went straight off to Pelham, offering him his allegiance, and his interest, and his boroughs on certain terms. The position was simple enough. 'As I was now,' wrote Dodington, 'entirely free from engagements, I was sincerely desirous of Mr. Pelham's favour and friendship, if he would accept of my friendship and attachment ; if, then, he would accept of my services, he might, *under proper conditions*, command my interest, and in that case nobody would be more welcome to me at Weymouth than Mr. Ellis.'

Cynicism cannot go further than this. Of principles, opinions, patriotic aims, Dodington knew nothing. Pelham had a place or two to sell, and Dodington had a handful of boroughs—the currency which could purchase them. And the old comedy went on again, transferred to another stage. Both parties were willing to do business, and a bargain might easily have been struck, if only the King had not been obdurate. He was not a politician in the true sense. He had been affronted by Dodington, and he was very angry. He would not forgive the man who had encouraged his son in rebellion. When Dodington appeared at Court, the King asked Pelham what brought him thither. Pelham replied, ' to show his duty, and that he wished to live in his favour.' ' No,' said the King, ' there has been too much of that already.'

So the conversations continued without any result for some three years. Dodington was truculent and obsequious by turns. When the Princess taxed him with disloyalty to her, he said that ' in politicks we must act in some way or other, and we cannot cease action for a time and then take it up again.' That such a man should use the word ' action ' at all is absurd, and yet why should he underrate his services, when he would ' undertake to chuse five members for the present Ministry without putting them to a shilling expense or desiring them to make a single tide-waiter ' ?

Pelham escaped from Dodington's importunity by death alone, and left him and his grievances and his threats to his brother, the Duke of Newcastle. The Duke and Dodington were perfectly well matched. Each wanted to get as much as he could out of the other. The Duke knew how handsome Dodington's proceedings had been, and Dodington blandly reminded the Duke that ' there were few who could give the King six members for nothing.' For nothing, said he ! Yet for nothing he would stir neither hand nor foot. Every ' action ' which he performed had its price, and mounted in value like the Sibylline books. He was not one to forget ' marketable ware.' When, to serve the King, he took part in the Bridgewater election, the sum of money he had spent there rose in the course of a few months from £2000 to £3400, and finally reached the respectable figure of £4000.

And then, as if to increase the value of his sacrifice, he had the impudence to deplore the corruption of the voters. He solemnly regrets the days which were ' spent in the infamous and disagreeable compliance with the low habits of venal wretches.' Thus the politician always deplores the manners and morals of the electors, whom his own greed and cunning have corrupted. The hypocrisy is an uglier sin than the greed, and you may match them both at elections recorded since. The candidates flatter the venal wretches on the platform at the top of their voice, and then in the intimacy of colleagues paint them in their true colours. As for Dodington, he liked neither the wretches nor their low habits. He gladly tolerated them because, with an energy which in another cause might have been admirable, he was determined to make some figure in life. ' I earnestly hoped it might be under your protection,' he told Newcastle, ' but if that could not be, I must make some figure ; what it would be, I could not determine yet ; I must look round a little, and consult my friends, but some figure I was resolved to make.' To us it seems remarkable that these two plotters could meet day after day and bargain and chaffer, without laughing in one another's face. Yet they were gravely solemn about it, and I do not suppose that Dodington smiled, even when the Duke of Newcastle kissed him !

Dodington did not cut the figure he wished to cut, and Newcastle so far failed to appease the placeman that he was presently charged with ' weakness, meanness, cowardice, and baseness.' At last the King, upon whose death Dodington had speculated for a quarter of a century, died, and Dodington was raised by his successor to the peerage as Lord Melcombe. His childish vanity expressed itself with childish exuberance, and the honour, enjoyed for too brief a space, inspired him, no doubt, to compose the best copy of verses that ever he wrote. After all, the policy of unenlightened egoism which he had pursued for fifty years had served him well enough, and as he looked back on his career, he saw and put into words what had always been his true aim :

> ' Love thy country, wish it well,
> Not with too intense a care,
> 'Tis enough that when it fell
> Thou its ruin didst not share.'

We can almost forgive Dodington all his follies, all his vices for those few words, ' not with too intense a care,' in which are summed up, with an exquisite touch of unconscious humour, the selfishness of his kind. In brief, he was a politician, not a patriot nor a leader of a forlorn hope. And they err who say that we must forgive him, because he should not be tried by the standard of our time. The standard of his day has been the standard of politicians ever since. Whether we like it or not, we are generally governed by Dodingtons, whose care of their country is not ' too intense,' and who agree with their master that ' it is all for quarter-day.'

LORD CASTLEREAGH

IN August 1822 Lord Castlereagh died by his
own hand—worn out in the service of his
country. And his name and fame are but now
faintly emerging from the mist of detraction in which
the pens and tongues of evil or foolish men have
enwrapped them. The Whigs, whose rancour never
dies, have pursued the memory of Castlereagh with
a tireless fury, as though he was still present to fight
for his country in the first line of defence. They
hated him because he loved Great Britain, while they
loved Great Britain's enemies. It is impossible, for
instance, to imagine the frailest bond of sympathy
which might have united Castlereagh and Fox. The
men of letters reproached him because he did not
mistake a showy eloquence for the end and aim of
statesmanship, because he knew well that it was a
greater offence to condone murder than to mix a
metaphor. The poets, the most resolute of his foes,
insulted and maligned him, each according to his own
whim and fancy. To Byron, Castlereagh was a
monster, because his energy and foresight had been
the undoing of Byron's hero, Napoleon, or because he
didn't approve of Castlereagh's management of the
English tongue. Shelley saw in him a determined

enemy of the emotional anarchy which served him for
a political creed.   When he ' met Murder on the way,
he had a mask like Castlereagh,' and it mattered not
to him that the Minister of his hatred had saved the
country.   As M. Capefigue, a Frenchman and
Castlereagh's loyal panegyrist, asked many years ago :
' Fallait-il laisser périr l'Angleterre pour plaire à des
poètes ?   Fallait-il seconder les desseins des brûleurs
de métiers et des voleurs de maisons ? '   To M. Capefigue's question a tardy answer has been given, and
even in this time of revolutionary excesses the debts
which wise and decent citizens owe to Castlereagh
are at last remembered.

I

Robert Stewart, Lord Castlereagh, was born in
1769, and having been educated at St. John's College,
Cambridge, went early into politics.   He was no more
than one-and-twenty when he was elected by County
Down to the Irish Parliament, after a contest, long
since legendary, which is said to have cost his family
sixty thousand pounds, and which impoverished his
father until the end of his life.   Four years later he
was sent to Westminster, and seconded, in 1795, the
Address in our English House of Commons.   Marked
out for preferment from the beginning, he was
appointed in 1797, by Lord Camden, Keeper of the
Privy Seal in Ireland, did Pelham's work as Chief
Secretary until Pelham's retirement a year later, when
he was himself appointed Chief Secretary at the age

of twenty-eight.   Not for a moment did he under-
estimate the burden of responsibility laid upon him.
He had a clear prophetic vision of events.   He knew
well what lay in store for Ireland and for him.   France
had declared her aim to be the tyrant of Europe, and
Ireland, after her wont, had knit herself in the closest
ties with England's enemy.   It was Castlereagh's
duty to suppress by all means in his power the rebellion
which threatened the peace, the very existence of
Ireland.   The united Irishmen were a powerful body
of men.   They were said by some to exceed 50,000 in
number, and they included rebels of all ages and classes.
By a prudent policy, at once suave and stern, Lord
Castlereagh put an end to the revolt.   He did not
fear to take repressive measures, whenever he thought
they were necessary for the safety of the country.   He
was an untiring watch-dog upon the rebels.   He
proved a talent of just vigilance which was a constant
check to the disloyal.   His system of intelligence was
perfect.   He discovered the plans of the rebels before
they were become active, and by his grasp of detail
showed to the world the great administrator that he
was.   On the one hand, he was in communication
with Emmet and his friends ;   on the other, the projects of the French Directory for the invasion of
Ireland never escaped him.   And it was mainly due
to his energy and watchfulness that the rebellion of
1798 was finally suppressed.

Never did he underrate the necessity and the difficulty of the enterprise.   Looking beyond Ireland to

the shores of France, he was convinced that the pacifi-
cation of Ireland was the first stage on the long hard
road of victory over France. So long as the soldiers
of the enemy were permitted to land upon Irish soil,
so long could the rebels, led and enforced by the
ambitious tyranny of the French, strike a foul blow
at England's heart. While he never ceased to follow
the movements of Napper Tandy and Wolfe Tone,
he did not neglect such help as his English colleagues
might afford. He insisted that England should aid
Ireland with men and arms. 'The force that will
be disposable,' he wrote to Pitt, ' when the troops from
England arrive, cannot fail to dissipate every alarm ;
and I consider it peculiarly advantageous that we shall
owe our security entirely to the interposition of Great
Britain. I have always been apprehensive of that
false confidence which might arise from an impression
that security has been obtained by our own exertions.
Nothing would tend so much to make the public mind
impracticable with a view to that future settlement,
without which we can never hope for any permanent
tranquillity.'

Stout fighter though he was, Castlereagh was
always the friend of clemency. He was in favour of
a generous amnesty while the rebellion was still unbroken, and was thwarted in his amiable design by the
British Government. When the civil war was
practically at an end, and when the battle had been
fought at Vinegar Hill, he wrote in a congratulatory
letter, addressed to General Lake, these wise words :

' I consider the rebels as now in your power, and I feel assured that your treatment of them will be such as will make them sensible of their crimes, as well as of the authority of government. It would be unwise and contrary, I know, to your feelings to drive the wretched people, who are mere instruments in the hands of the more wicked, to despair. The leaders are just objects of punishment.' And yet Castlereagh, like all those brave men who do not shrink from the suppression of massacre and arson, has been held up to the reprobation of the world. He has been set on the pillory which the Whigs keep for honest and courageous men. Twenty years after the event Lord Brougham, in a debate on the state of the nation, did not scruple to repeat ancient calumnies, invented by worthless and interested rebels. ' A man who has practised torture on men,' said Brougham, falsely suggesting that Castlereagh had callously witnessed ' the scenes of horror ' of the '98, ' had obtained a bill of indemnity for all transactions, of which such cruelty had formed a part.' Presently Brougham, in his *Historical Sketches*, told another story, either because the calumny no longer served his turn, or because he had forgotten it. ' Lord Castlereagh,' thus he wrote, ' uniformly and strenuously set his face against the atrocities committed in Ireland ; and to him more than perhaps any one else is to be attributed the termination of the system stained with blood.' Lord Brougham would have done better had he never brought the false charge, or having brought it, had made a speedy and public meal of his own words.

When the rebellion was quelled at last, the act of Union became a plain necessity. Since the end of English policy was the defeat of France, Pitt's imperative duty was to make one kingdom of Great Britain and Ireland. Thus only could he ensure that sense of security at home which was indispensable if our arms were to triumph abroad. Once more Castlereagh was set to work, and he displayed the same vigour in promoting the Union which he had displayed in quelling the rebellion. Now it must be remembered that the problem of the Union as Castlereagh faced it in 1799 was not the same problem which has since baffled our interested politicians. It was the Protestants who were then in most violent opposition to the proposed change. The young barristers of the Four Courts, violent and vociferous, clamoured against it. The owners of the boroughs feared that the Union would put them out of pocket. Many of the Irish peers, deaf though they might be to the noisy propaganda of United Ireland, feared the loss of prestige and independence. The Catholics, on the other hand, cared not very deeply which way the matter went. They had had no part in Grattan's Parliament, and were not profoundly moved by the prospect of enfranchisement. Nor did the cry of what by a grim irony was called 'Catholic emancipation' find a loud echo in English hearts. Though both Castlereagh and Pitt were in favour of it, its acceptance would not have been easy.   If it had come before the Union, the Catholics would have supported what has since been known as Home Rule, for the mere pleasure of having their will of the Protestants. Had emancipation and Union gone hand-in-hand, the Protestants would assuredly have rejected them both. And if the stumbling-blocks which lay in the path of emancipation had been smaller than they were, the opposition of the King would have made progress along that path impossible.   It is unlikely also that, had emancipation accompanied or immediately followed Union, the course of events would have been much changed.   The Irish are always eloquent in talking of what ' might have been.'   But whatever was made no difference to the irreconcilables, and it was always a pleasure for those, who failed to govern themselves, to invent new crimes for England.

The difficulties of the business did but encourage Castlereagh to a greater vigour.   Opposition set a finer edge upon his temper.   While he kept in view the true aim of his policy—the Union of the Kingdom and the security of the Empire—he neglected not the smallest detail.   He wrote innumerable letters ;   he paid and received countless visits ;   and never once did he despair of ultimate success.   His papers bear eloquent testimony both to his tact and his assiduity. He was under no illusion about the difficulties which he had to overcome.   His friends were too deeply sincere to put him off with palatable fictions.   ' The tide of opposition to this measure,' wrote Dr. Duigenan,

M.P. for Armagh, to him, ' runs so strong at present
in this city (Dublin), that some of the first and most
popular characters who are perfectly convinced of the
expediency, nay, almost of the necessity, of the
measure, are afraid openly to proclaim their opinions,
convinced that they would, by so doing, lose that
popularity which they may in proper season use for
purposes beneficent to Church and State.' Castlereagh was unperturbed. When on 22nd January the
Bill for the Union was thrown out, and Dublin was
illuminated, Castlereagh took it all as an incentive to
further activity, knowing well that the question of the
Union would be asked again, and that pertinacity
would ensure success. Month by month the policy
of Union became more urgent. France was preparing fresh armaments to be used against the English
in Ireland at the very moment when the cause which
Pitt and Castlereagh had at heart was imperilled by
levity and dissension. Castlereagh insisted still upon
continuity of thought and purpose. ' Nothing,'
wrote he to the Duke of Portland, ' but an established
conviction that the English Government will never
lose sight of the Union till it is carried will give the
measure a chance of success.' Neither Castlereagh
nor the British Government lost sight of the measure,
and it passed the Irish House by a majority of sixty-
five on 7th June 1800.

The security of the kingdom had not been attained
without promises given, which now clamoured for
fulfilment. There had been much talk of pensions

and promotions and steps in the peerage, and Castlereagh, always a target for the arrows of disappointed
Whigs, has been freely charged with political corruption. That he took such steps as were needful for
the success of Pitt's design is true enough ; and even
had all the charges brought against him been true, his
defence would have been easy. The urgency of the
business was beyond dispute or cavil. The Union
must be made, or England must perish. The gathering force of France was a constant menace, and her
determination to invade Ireland increased with increasing strength. Not many days after the Union was
established, Castlereagh received from Mr. Pitt's
secretary news which explained his action. ' A Swiss
gentleman, lately arrived from France,' said Mr.
Cooke, ' gives this account that Bonaparte is adored ;
everything is plentiful but money ; that Paris is all
gaiety ; that they talk little of politics. . . . Bonaparte's preparations for his campaign were kept as
secret and were as extensive as possible ; that he has
another army of reserve as numerous as that which is
victorious.' These facts, long familiar to Castlereagh,
were a complete justification for what Castlereagh had
done. He had furthered the Union not to illustrate a
method of politics, nor because he had, as his enemies
have foolishly declared, a natural love of oppression.
In thought, in speech, in action he had been inspired
by a wise and just fear of France, whose intentions
were hidden from him as little as her prosperity. So
hazardous, indeed, was the situation that he had used

such pressure as statesmen are wont to use in difficult circumstances, and he had used it not to help an ambitious Minister but to save the country.

He himself has explained what he did, with the quiet understatement characteristic of him. 'What has been done,' he wrote to Lord Camden ten days after the Union, ' has proceeded from the best view we could form of the necessities of our Government ; and I feel assured that the King's Ministers, in reviewing it after the object is attained, will not be disposed to canvass upon the cold grounds of abstract convenience in point of patronage, much less with any disposition to avoid the charge of having made the favours of the Crown, in an unusual extent, auxiliary to the measure.' The King's Ministers, well satisfied with what had been done in Ireland, did their best to fulfil the promises of Cornwallis and Castlereagh. It was beyond their power to protect their faithful friends and supporters against rancour and detraction. The amiable Lord Brougham was early in the field with vague charges of bribery and corruption, though, as Castlereagh's brother protested, one objection to the Act of Union was that it put an end to a vast deal of buying and selling votes and seats. A letter from the Marquess Cornwallis to Lord Wellesley, written on 3rd April 1800, sets the matter in a clear light. ' We have hitherto carried all our questions,' writes Cornwallis, ' by a majority of between forty and fifty ; but I am sorry to say that it is an unwilling majority, dragged out with difficulty to vote by the orders of borough proprietors who brought them into Parliament, and detesting the measure which blasts their hopes of obtaining those little *douceurs* which have so long been enjoyed by the members of the Irish House of Commons. The *great commanding interests* which have so handsomely supported us remain firm and unshaken, and I trust that it will not be in the power of clamour, folly, or treason to prevent our ultimate success.'

II

Thus the first part of Castlereagh's trilogy ended in complete triumph. He had accomplished without fuss and without clamour the two tasks which had been set him—the suppression of the rebellion, and the Union of Ireland and Great Britain. His reputation had marvellously increased, and Pitt, who was always quick to recognise a practical statesman, saw at once how valuable his support would be in the United House of Commons. One thing only threatened the wish and the hope of Pitt. An English peerage had been offered to Castlereagh's father by the King, and thus one single life protected Castlereagh from sudden banishment to the House of Lords. There was much argument and many exchanges of views. The highest compliment was paid to Castlereagh by the general desire of the Ministers that he should run no risk of departure from the House of Commons. It seemed almost as though Lord Londonderry's accession to an English peerage would involve a national crisis. Mr. Pitt's secretary wrote to Castlereagh in grave insistent terms. ' I am almost persuaded,' said he, ' that you will be obliged to postpone your father's peerage. No man was ever so flatteringly pressed to decline honours. The real fact is that they hope you will make the same figure and take the same lead which you have done in Ireland, and they sadly want some character on whom business may repose. Mr. Pitt's health is certainly equivocal ; his personal contest with Bonaparte may distress him should he be driven to peace. Windham is ingeniously imprudent ; Dundas is retiring ; Ryder is an invalid ; Lord Hawkesbury not leading talents ; Canning neither rank nor authority, and has not yet shown himself a man of business.' It was flattery indeed to a young man of thirty, and the problem was happily solved by Lord Londonderry admitting that ' His Majesty's interests might best be promoted by his not having that distinction at present conferred upon him.' I know not which more to wonder at—the honour done to the son, or the father's abnegation.

At the outset the father's abnegation met with scant reward. The troublesome question of Catholic emancipation suspended for a while the triumph of the son. When the King, in fear of violating his coronation oath, refused to admit the Catholics to the franchise, and denounced Castlereagh for a Jacobin, Pitt had no choice but resignation, and Castlereagh resigned with him. For two years only was he absent from office, and then, in 1802, overpersuaded by Pitt, he took his seat in the Cabinet as President of the

East India Board of Control. Though he served under Addington, he remained the friend of Pitt, and was able to press the views of the retired statesman upon the Prime Minister, whom he distrusted, and the Cabinet, which he should himself have controlled. On the death of William Pitt, his friend and leader, Castlereagh became a stout opponent of Grenville's ministry, and returned to the Cabinet as Secretary of War when Portland was head of the Government. While at the War Office, Castlereagh kept one single-minded hope, one firm purpose before him—the defeat of Napoleon.   His somewhat narrow intellect had the quality of its defect, a rare power of concentration. He thought of nothing, worked for nothing, save the victory of Great Britain ; and when at last success rewarded his great effort, he had the satisfaction of ridding Europe of the menace which had hung over it, like a black shadow, for more than twenty years.

At the outset he reshaped the Army, which he increased by volunteers from the militia as well as by recruits ; and so well did his plan work that in 1808 he was able to put in the field a force of 532,000 men. Though, like other civilian Secretaries of War, he made mistakes, and irritated by his frigid despatches the vain susceptibilities of certain generals, the lines of his policy were truly drawn, and converged to the great end which he held in view.   He supported whole-heartedly the seizure of the Danish Fleet after the negotiations of Tilsit, and thus prevented the Baltic from becoming what Napoleon had designed

it to be—a French lake.   And if the expedition to
Walcheren failed, it was not by the fault of Castlereagh,
but by the supine inaction and disobedience of Chatham.
Had Chatham carried out the clear orders of the
Minister, success had been certain.   The Minister's
chief objective was Antwerp, and Chatham, by attacking only Flushing, gave Napoleon the chance of
strengthening Antwerp.   Disease, fighting on the
side of France, did the rest, and Castlereagh, who,
had Chatham succeeded, would have yielded the glory
to the commander of the expedition, has been asked
to bear the burden of failure alone.

The instructions which he addressed to Lord
Chatham are his best vindication.   ' Your Lordship,'
he wrote, ' will consider the operation in question as,
in its execution, more immediately directed against
the fleet and arsenals of France in the Scheldt.   The
complete success of the operation would include the
capture or destruction of the whole of the enemy's
ships, either building at Antwerp or afloat in the
Scheldt, the entire destruction of their yards and
arsenals at Antwerp, Terneuse, and Flushing, and the
rendering, if possible, the Scheldt no longer navigable
for ships of war.'   Chatham, by leaving Antwerp un-
attacked, forced Castlereagh's excellent plan to mis-
carry, and the duel with Canning, which followed,
drove the Secretary of War into retirement for two
years.   Meanwhile he had begun to make a reality
of Pitt's prophecy that Napoleon would be beaten by
a nation in arms, probably in Spain, and had done his

F

best to equip and support the expedition to the Penin-
sula.   His wise judgment of men had persuaded him
at last to put Arthur Wellesley in command, and the
success of the campaign, which he had planned and
designed, played a large part in the undoing of Napoleon.
As in detail his policy was wisely planned, so in its
larger lines it manifested a true statesmanship.   He
understood clearly that England single-handed was no
match for Napoleon, and he did his best to bring
together the forces of the Allies, that they might
combine by land and sea against the common enemy.
The task was difficult, since the jealousy of friends may
be a greater danger than the pertinacity of foes.   But
the tact and patience of Castlereagh were sufficient for
the strain.   He was ready now to be firm in exaction,
now to concede what was not of the highest importance, and his diplomatic skill held together a Coalition
which in hands less deft might have broken down
under the strain.

III

And this brings us to the third part of the trilogy of
Castlereagh.   When he returned to power in 1812,
as Foreign Secretary and leader of the House of
Commons, he performed what many think his greatest
services to the country.   Henceforth he was, as M.
Thiers called him, 'England herself in the camp of
the Coalition.'   By a strange irony the man who has
since been universally insulted spoke then with the
voice not of a government but of a country.   When he
came back to England from Vienna in 1814, the House

of Commons rose to do him honour, and even Mr.
Whitbread silenced for a moment the voice of his
malice. Meanwhile he had kept one dominant
object before him, to hold the Coalition together.
He knew well that Napoleon could be defeated only
by unanimity, and while he did his utmost to strengthen
existing alliances, he was always alive to the importance
of detaching the Powers still friendly to France from
their allegiance. With the greatest adroitness he
secured the neutrality of Sweden, and not only did he
gather the members of the Coalition together ; he
inspired them to an activity equalling his own. He
procured them subsidies ; he supplied them with
arms, with clothes, with all the material that is indispensable to victory. Thus he became, in a sense, the
direct personal rival of Napoleon on the Continent,
and it is the highest tribute to his firmness and his
judgment that the Europe which he found at war he
left in peace.

His mere appearance at a Congress was an assurance
of its success. At Chaumont, in 1813, he exacted
a pledge from the Allies to continue the war against
Napoleon until it was brought to a victorious end ;
at Châtillon, in 1814, he compelled the Powers,
eager in dissension, to establish a lasting peace among
themselves. Yet, much as he loved peace, he would
make no paltry sacrifice to preserve it. He was
always a man of courage, not afraid to take the
risks of statesmanship. When Napoleon was safe at
Elba, Alexander, with a dramatic gesture, put his

finger upon the map of Poland, and exclaimed *c'est à moi*. Castlereagh, ready to face another war rather than leave the Russians masters of Europe, did not hesitate to make clear to Alexander what the consequences would be of his ambition, and Alexander was prudent enough to submit. And it was after Waterloo that Castlereagh reached the highest point of his career. The defeat of Napoleon, in which his Irish policy had been the first step, had left Europe broken in pieces, and it was Castlereagh's business to put the pieces together again. When he went to Vienna he left behind all thought of vengeance, all desire of profit for England. His chief aim was to preserve a proper balance of power, and he knew that this could be preserved only by refraining to punish France, and bringing her back to the old limits which were drawn before Napoleon began his career of conquest. Thus only, he knew, could the peace of Europe endure, and to this end he subordinated the interests of his own as well as of other countries.

Since Castlereagh's time we have seen a peace contrived by ' plain men.' One of the plainest of them boasted that he would not fall into the errors which had (he thought) disgraced Castlereagh. The plain men are not quite so arrogant as they were, and their bungling, the bungling of ignorant men—for plainness is ignorance—has not achieved the results achieved by the wisdom of Castlereagh, who assured Europe half a century's rest from war, and left it after a violent contest almost without rancour. Now

Castlereagh succeeded in these aims because, in the first place, he was a practical statesman. 'He was that rare phenomenon,' said Lord Salisbury, 'a practical man of the highest order, who yet did not by that fact forfeit his title to be considered a man of genius.' He kept always within the limits of moderation. He did not aim at one target and hit another. He had striven to free Europe from a tyrant, and he was determined not to involve it in another and a worse despotism. In the second place, he was not of those who want to keep a finger in every pie. It was never his desire to control the affairs of others. He cared not how France or any other nation managed its business, so long as it kept the peace. He declared again and again that Great Britain would have nothing to do with a system which seemed 'to lead to the creation of general government in Europe, with a superintending Directory, destructive of all correct notions of internal sovereign authority.' So he was the enemy of all conferences summoned for no particular reason, and he bitterly disliked the habit, popular again in our own time, of regarding foreign policy as a kind of travelling circus.

Opposed wisely and unalterably to interference with the affairs of others, he looked upon the Holy Alliance, the offspring of Alexander's fevered brain, as a piece of 'sublime mysticism and nonsense.' When Alexander, who regarded himself as a Russian Messiah, concocted his famous scheme with M. de Krüdener, Castlereagh would have none of it. He saw that it would result in perpetual intervention and perpetual war. If it were to succeed in imposing its views upon a reluctant world, it would need to keep an efficient army, ready to march whither it was ordered at an hour's notice. It would ensure a series of petty quarrels which could be settled only by the sword, and would keep the peace, so long and ardently desired by Castlereagh, away from Europe for ever. Yet he was at great pains not to hurt the susceptibilities of Alexander, with whom at Vienna it was necessary that he should work harmoniously. And he put his proposal by with a gentle irony. 'The benign principles of the alliance of the 26th of September 1815,' he wrote, 'may be considered as constituting the European system in matter of political conscience. It would, however, be derogatory to this solemn act of the sovereigns to mix its discussion with the ordinary diplomatic obligations, which bind state to state, and which are to be looked for alone in the treaties which have been concluded in the accustomed form.' Thus he administered a welcome piece of flattery to Alexander's self-esteem, and made it clear that for Great Britain, at any rate, the Holy Alliance would remain a pious, inactive aspiration.

In truth, he opposed every design which he thought might interfere with peace. To the nonsense which has since been talked about the 'rights' of small nationalities he was wholly indifferent. Had the foolish scheme of 'self-determination,' which will cause rivers of blood to flow presently, been put before

him, he would have brushed it aside indignantly.   He
did not think that a common speech made half a dozen
tribes, alien from one another in blood, into a single
nation.   He would have scouted the proposal that a
mob of men, mixed in race as in language, should be
held to be an indivisible state merely because a majority
of them wished it.   His practical intellect persuaded
him to look askance at the views of dreamers and
sentimentalists.   He approved of nothing which he
thought might interrupt the newly-made peace.   He
treated France, after the war, with a kindliness which
some of the Allies found hard to bear.   He saved
Paris from destruction, while at the same time he
insisted that she should return the works of art which
Napoleon's despoiling hand had collected from his
foes.   When France urged her claim to be admitted
to the Grand Alliance, Castlereagh was ready to assent,
despite the opposition of Russia and Austria ; for, said
he, if you exclude France from your councils, she will
become the centre of a separate alliance of her own.
Thus he seems, in his wisdom, a pure intelligence in
human shape, working without rancour, without
thought of aggrandisement or revenge, and as he was
hated for this impassibility in his own time, so he has
been maligned for it ever since.

IV

When at last the war was over and peace abroad
assured, Castlereagh did his best to restore peace at
home.   The troubled years which followed the fall

of Napoleon demanded a strong hand, and fortunately
the Government, of which Castlereagh was a member,
was not intimidated either by rebellious deeds or by
subversive speeches.   The Six Acts which followed
Peterloo were useful and well-timed.   They inflicted no hardship upon the peaceful citizen, and they
made the way of the transgressor harder to travel.
There is no right inherent in the 'people' of anarchy,
and so long as the law-breaker is uncontrolled, the
'people' itself, not so sacred as it is said to be, suffers
far more acutely than the simple citizens, who are
excluded by their worth and thrift from its privileges.
Yet it is Castlereagh's just suppression of disorder that
has brought the wildest curses upon him, and gives us
a clue to the persistent misunderstanding of his
character.   He had not the obvious virtues of the
politician.   He neither loved nor sought popularity.
It was not his purpose to do what would please others,
but what in his own mind he knew was for the good
of the country.   He appeared to the general cold and
passionless, and this impression was not lessened—
perhaps it was enhanced—by the grace and dignity
of his bearing.   The excitements and perturbations to
which smaller men fall easy victims did not touch his
stern tranquillity.   As Lord Salisbury writes in a
memorable passage : 'No tinge of that enthusiastic
temper which leads men to overhunt a beaten enemy,
to drive a common cause to excess, to swear allegiance
to a formula, or to pursue an impracticable ideal, ever
threw a shadow on Castlereagh's serene impassive

intelligence.' That is perfectly true, and it helps to
explain why those who regard politics as a branch of
drama look down upon Castlereagh with a fool's
contempt. The long struggle between Castlereagh
and Canning, which ended in a duel, was a contest of
temperaments. Castlereagh was a statesman, and no
more. Canning was a wit and a poet and a rhetorician
besides. The set of a phrase was of higher importance to him than the wisdom of a measure ; and it is
perhaps not surprising that, in overestimating his own
talents, he should fail to appreciate the sounder judgment, the quieter method of speech, which were his
rival's. They were by nature and training incompatible ; and though it is plain that Canning came far
below Castlereagh in scruple, it does not matter much
what was the immediate cause of the duel—Canning's
readiness to sacrifice Sir John Moore, or his treachery
to his colleague. The quarrel was foreordained, and
there is an end of it.

Another cause for the misunderstanding of Castlereagh is the common vice of condemning a statesman
because he does not possess qualities to which he has
never aspired. It is idle to repeat that Castlereagh was
the best Minister of Foreign Affairs in his time. You
are met by the irrelevant assertion that he was a bad
actor. The truth is that Castlereagh was a poor
speaker and an indifferent writer. His speeches were
verbose and without ornament. His despatches,
according to the wont of such things, are indubitably
dull. And these objections seem to me to be inapposite.

We do not choose the managers of our banks for their eloquence or their wit. Our great captains of industry are absolved for the absence of other talents if only they are complete masters of their business. And why should we set up for a statesman a false and artificial standard ? Windham said that Pitt could deliver a King's speech at a minute's notice, and Castlereagh's method of exposition was less briskly exhilarating than Pitt's. Yet I have sought in vain for the mixed metaphors and ridiculous images with which his words—written and spoken—are said by the wits to abound. All that can be said is that Castlereagh had no interest whatever in the niceties of literary style. He was above all things a man of action, plain of speech and wise in counsel. There is no statesman of his time to whom England owes a deeper debt of gratitude. He saved Europe from the oppression of a despot, and he did more than any other to contrive at Vienna a just and lasting peace. He gave his life to his country, and died by his own hand an exhausted man of fifty-three. It does not, then, matter vastly that his literary style failed to win the approval of Moore and Byron ; and it is all the more necessary to remember his gallant life and his hapless death, because his career illustrated the rare and noble statesmanship of which we too often stand in bitter need.

A MAKER OF COLONIES

IT is not surprising that Edward Gibbon Wakefield
has been neglected for more than half a century,
for Edward Gibbon Wakefield was a prophet, and
prophets are commonly without honour not only in
their own but in every other country. Moreover,
the knowledge which he had of the future was a
practical knowledge ; he knew the means whereby
his fancies would be turned into facts ; and when the
event proved the clearness of his vision, envious ones
were not wanting to resent his accurate judgment.
To-day the old animosities are falling into forgetfulness ; the opposition evoked by Wakefield's sincerity
perished long ago ; and at last a generation of imperial
enthusiasts has arisen, which honourably believes that
our dominions are our greatest glory, and which
sees in Wakefield the far-sighted statesman, whose
clairvoyance made possible the prosperity of the many
kingdoms oversea.

Wakefield was no mere politician. He was a
natural prey to the manifold contrasts and contra-
dictions which make for enterprise. An economist
with a taste for splendour, a Quaker beset with a
reckless levity, an hereditary philanthropist determined
before all things to better his own fortune, he ran upon

such shoals of adventure and disgrace as would have
foundered a less buoyant and courageous bark than his
own. Born in 1796 of a family given over to the
practice of benevolence, he was guided in his early
steps by the hardest, flattest-footed pedants who ever
worshipped the ideal of misery—Francis Place and
James Mill. Their influence was light upon him,
since his first employment was in the diplomatic
service, where he speedily learned the charm of fashion
and extravagance. He followed the tradition of his
family in making a youthful and surreptitious marriage.
His father was first married at seventeen, and afterwards contracted a secret alliance in Paris. One of
his brothers ran off with an Indian princess. And of
all the Wakefields it was Edward Gibbon who most
notoriously distinguished himself in the field of matri-
mony. He eloped with Eliza Susan Pattle, a wealthy
ward of Chancery, before he was of full age, and he
carried through the enterprise with considerable dash
and ingenuity. The lady was guarded not only by a
vigilant mother, but by two jealous uncles, so that
flight was difficult and dangerous. Wakefield overcame all obstacles ; he pursued his sweetheart to
Tunbridge Wells, lulled the uncles' suspicions by a
feigned interest in cock-fighting, and on a summer
morning hired two carriages, in one of which he drove
off with the lady, while a pair of dummies seated in the
other diverted the pursuit. Of course he escaped clear
away, married his Eliza, overpersuaded the Lord
Chancellor, and at last won the enduring affection of

his mother-in-law. That his conduct was influenced by greed and ambition is certain; it is also certain that he made whatever amend was possible to fidelity and affection; indeed, it was but the premature death of his wife that drove Wakefield back upon a career of bustle and intrigue; and his subsequent offence may be easily condoned, since the most poignant grief cannot tame a high-spirited boy of twenty-four.

At twenty-four, then, Edward Gibbon Wakefield was dividing his time between Genoa and Paris, an irresponsible *attaché*, enjoying, according to his own phrase, the most highly cultivated society in Europe. He was gay, handsome, careless, and witty; exquisite in his dress, eager in his pleasures, yet withal untiring in ambition. His purpose was Parliament and a political career. He would enter the House, give a loyal support to Mr. Canning, and prove that the rising generation was neither venal nor treasonable. There is something in his youthful spirit which recalls the more dazzling brilliance of Disraeli. 'We are enthusiasts,' he cries out, with a confidence which the author of *Vivian Grey* echoed a few years later; 'to be sure we are! We commenced writing on politics because we are political enthusiasts; because we are sick of the dull, calculating, measured trash of one set of newspapers, and the prejudiced, senseless, savage violence of others. . . . Enthusiasts indeed! And is it not high time that enthusiasts should appear in the only cause that is worthy enthusiasm? We spurn the mawkish affectation which supposes that England has seen her brightest days of civilisation, prosperity, and glory.' How young it is—young with the eternal justice and generosity of youth ! And thus, his head packed with dreams of patriotism, he believed that all things were possible to him ; and even the Treasury Bench seemed but a saunter to his courageous energy.

One thing only was lacking—money. And by hook or by crook money must be found, not so much to gratify personal vanity, as to give a patriot the chance of serving his country. Already he had proved the ease and profit of elopement, and with the aid of his family he resolved once more upon a runaway match. History does not contain a stranger episode than Wakefield's second flight, and it is the stranger because not merely did his stepmother—as yet unacknowledged by her husband, after the custom of the family—herself select the victim, but his brother William was an actual accomplice in the crime. The plot was laid with deliberate cunning ; nothing was left to chance ; and it was only the harsh interference of the law which baulked the reckless Wakefield of his prey.

Now, on a certain March morning in 1826, a post-chaise drew up at the door of a girls' school near Liverpool. A letter was presented to the mistress declaring that the mother of Miss Ellen Turner was dying, and that she requested her daughter's instant presence. The schoolmistress, suspecting nothing, bade the girl depart, and, in accordance with the letter's behest, gave no reason for the hurried journey. A few miles from Liverpool the chaise was met by Wakefield and his brother, who accompanied the girl to Carlisle, and there told her that her father, being on the brink of ruin, could be saved only by her speedy marriage with her adventurous companion. With no resource but compliance, she crossed the frontier to Gretna Green, where the ceremony was hastily gone through, and whence Wakefield and his stolen bride fled to Calais. When once his purpose was effected, Wakefield behaved with astounding moderation. He surrendered his captive to her friends without complaint ; he made a solemn declaration that ' she and he had been but as brother and sister,' and he was so far penitent as to confess that had another behaved so monstrously to his daughter he would have shot him. Nor was the incident without a touch of pathos. ' I would have made her love me,' said the greedy adventurer in perfect truth ; and when the ring, taken from her finger, was returned to him, ' I shall always keep it,' he replied ; ' they should have thrown it away.'

A monstrous outrage had been committed, and Wakefield, declining an opportunity of flight to America, returned to stand his trial with his brother and stepmother. A strange trial it was, indeed, and one which puzzled the ablest lawyers of the time. As Wakefield lifted every enterprise above the commonplace, so this squalid theft of a schoolgirl could not be punished without an Act of Parliament. Miss

Turner was an essential witness, yet, if the marriage were legal, she could not give evidence against her husband. The difficulty might have proved insoluble without the aid of the Commons ; when once the marriage was annulled there was no vestige of hope for Wakefield ; and he was condemned to three years' imprisonment in Newgate. And now were made manifest the true strength and nobility of his character. Never once did he think of ruin or defeat. He would expiate the wrong, and pick up a brilliant career from the gutter where he had thrown it. More than that, he would turn his disgrace to practical advantage : he would leave Newgate a sound statesman, upon whose word the whole country must rely.

At the outset he meditated a history of Newgate, and devoted himself with all his lively enthusiasm to the study of the prison whose door was closed upon him. The history was never written, but the fragment which actually got into print is among the most amazing pamphlets in the language. Whether you estimate its own merit or its ultimate effect, you cannot read *Punishment by Death in the Metropolis* without a surprised admiration. One thing is certain : had Wakefield chosen, he might have proved an accomplished man of letters. There are passages of melodrama, even of tragedy, in this shapeless pamphlet, which you can hardly match elsewhere in literature. Yes, and pages of ironic humour, too, which force a smile, even in the shadow of the tree. Who can forget the school of crime, and the villainous

instructor, who may have given Dickens a hint of
Fagin ?   Or the poor boys, condemned to the gallows,
from which their escape is certain, and none the less
proud of their rarely dignified position ?   'They have
just the same air of agreeable excitement and self-
importance,' writes Wakefield, 'for days before the
scene of respite takes place, as marks a Westminster
boy when he is about to be distinguished by acting in
public.'   It is hard, no doubt, upon the Westminster
boy, but then Wakefield had no love of his old school,
and at any rate the comparison is as apt as it is unexpected.   Then with what an admirable sense of fun
he describes the mock trials, enacted by the prisoners,
who imitate with real gusto the oddities of the counsel
whom they love and the judges whom they fear !
And above all, who shall exaggerate the splendid
horror of the condemned pew, tenanted on Black
Sunday by a returned convict, a mad sheep-stealer, a
clergyman of the Church of England, 'a miserable
old man in a tattered suit of black,' and a poor
youth, whose theft just passes the boundary of
five pounds, and whose 'hands tremble as they
hold the book upside down' ?   These passages
are burned into the memory, and prove by their
very persistence their author's rare and brilliant
talent.

Wakefield preferred action to words, and he purposely laid aside an artistic ambition, which he might
have gratified, for the inherited love of influence and
reform.   It is not for nothing that he was the cousin

of Elizabeth Fry ; and he doubtless forgot the eloquence of his pamphlet in the pride of its practical success. And well might he be proud, for few pieces of writing ever met with a speedier result. The evils which Wakefield's eloquence had exposed were presently reformed—the Draconian severity, which punished all crimes by death, and so brought the capital sentence into contempt ; the trivial habit of putting on the black cap before children, whose respite was assured, and who laughed in the dock at the judge's solemn jargon ; the infamous law which left the prosecution of criminals to private malice, and so contrived that a criminal might buy back his life from his victim. These evils are long since reformed and forgotten. Thus it is that we owe our system of public prosecutions to Wakefield's argument, and thus it is that a term of imprisonment suffered by a man of genius availed to reshape the code of England.

By his *Letter from Sydney*, Wakefield revealed a yet deeper talent, and again did his country a lasting service. From an artistic point of view, this pamphlet is admirable. Wakefield, of course, had never visited Australia, and his material was drawn from the conversation of convicts, and from the files of antiquated newspapers. And all who were familiar with our unhappy colony declared the *Letter from Sydney* a masterpiece of verisimilitude. It was written, said they, not within the dull dark walls of Newgate, but in the full sunshine of the Antipodes.

The country, the life, the settlers, were described with a light and graphic touch ; the author forgets neither the laziness of the men nor the beauty of the women. However, a picturesque presentation was not the object of Wakefield's pamphlet. He wrote the famous *Letter* from his cell in Newgate with the avowed purpose of reform. Our Australian colonies profited us nothing, and Wakefield set himself to discover the cause of failure. The cause was not far to seek. Australia was a magnificent country, where all men might take up a free, unbounded grant of land. There was no need of servitude, since every man was a landowner, and no man owed allegiance to anything or to anybody. Why then was prosperity withheld ? Why was this golden age besmirched with ruin and starvation ? Because where all men are masters the labourer exists not. Other young colonies had grown rich by the aid of slavery. In 1830 slavery was impossible, and Australia pined from excess of freedom. 'Capital without labour,' said Wakefield, ' is even more powerless than labour without capital.' Will you hew down trees with bank-notes, he asked in effect, or cleave the soil with sovereigns ? To the short-sighted rulers who had encouraged settlers by free grants of land one hope remained. The convict might be compelled to discharge the duties of a slave ; he too might be chained to the soil when he had laid aside his more irksome fetters. For this subterfuge Wakefield had a ready answer. ' If for every acre that may be appropriated here,' wrote the imagined colonist, ' there should be a conviction for felony in England, our prosperity would rest on a solid basis ; but, however earnestly we may desire it, we cannot expect that the increase of crime will keep pace with the spread of colonisation.' This excellent irony conveys a solid truth. Not even crime could take the place of slavery, and Australia became a Tom Tiddler's ground, where no labourer would condescend to pick up the gold.

The intelligence of the untravelled Wakefield discovered a perfect remedy. He suggested first that payment of money should be required in future for every grant of land, and second, that every acre of land thus granted should be liable to a tax, and that this tax should be employed in the free conveyance of British labourers to the colony. In these provisions we find the essence of the Wakefield system, which, devised in Newgate, changed the whole history of Australia, and which made a prosperous country of what would otherwise have relapsed into savagery from the mere impossibility of gathering wealth. That the new projects should have encountered opposition was inevitable. The old method of colonisation, pursued by British officialism, was still supreme, though it had lost us America ; and the Government's first anxiety was always to equip a fresh colony with governors, and clergy, and police. England, in fact, when Wakefield came to her rescue, was no more intelligent coloniser than the France of yesterday. But Wakefield, despite his stormy past, despite the fury of politicians, argued and intrigued until he had carried his point. And so it was that a casual breach of the law not only reformed our criminal code, but also inaugurated a wise and equitable system of colonisation.

Henceforth it was Edward Gibbon Wakefield who pulled the wires of every colonial enterprise, though a certain hypocrisy prevented the advertisement of his tarnished name, and for many years this eminent statesman was forced to work in secret. He received encouragement both from such respectable journals as the *Spectator* and from such politicians as Molesworth, Mill, and Lord Durham. Immediately on his enlargement he established the Colonisation Society, through which for some fifteen years he exercised a conspicuous influence, and with whose aid he ultimately founded South Australia. This was Wakefield's first great achievement, as its success was the first noble tribute to his memorable system. But the real founder reaped from the enterprise neither glory nor profit, and doubtless he was glad enough to turn his untiring energy to the new project for the colonisation of New Zealand. Of this project, too, Wakefield was the unseen and potent inspiration. His ingenuity it was which overcame the intrigues of Parliament and the criminal negligence of the Colonial Office. With Lord Durham's aid he formed the company which ultimately snatched New Zealand from alien hands, and which gave to England one of the most valuable among her colonies. But a graceless opposition

dogged every step of the new company. If Lord
Glenelg was supine, Lord Normanby was actively
hostile, and but for a brilliant stroke New Zealand
would probably have been lost for ever. The company
held a sudden meeting, declared a capital of £100,000,
equipped the *Tory*, which set sail with Wakefield's
son and brother William on board, and forced the
Government to accept the sovereignty of New
Zealand. Nor was all secure, even when the *Tory*
had left London with her guns, and her colonists, and
her money. A rumour went abroad that she would be
stopped at Plymouth, and then Wakefield performed
another signal service to New Zealand : he rode
post-haste to the west, warned the *Tory* against the
machinations of the Government, and the ship sailed
to the glory of England without giving a mean-souled
Minister the opportunity of a veto.

It is a strange and ungrateful history, this history of
the British colonies. Pedant arose after pedant on
the Treasury Bench, to declare that our colonies were
sufficient ; and hero after hero strove in obscurity to
extend the borders of his country's empire. Such
patriotism as Wakefield's shows no flaw. It was
disinterested, because his name might not be uttered ;
it was generously displayed, because without reward
Wakefield achieved what no highly flattered and highly
paid official could achieve without his counsel and
inspiration. He never complained of his suppression
nor grudged his service. When Lord Durham set
sail for Canada on his triumphant mission, it was to

Wakefield he looked for guidance, and it was Wakefield's name which might never be spoken in report
or state-paper. ' Oh no, we never mention him,' says
Lord Durham, in writing to his Minister, ' his name
is never heard.' And in all sincerity he adds : ' Really
if it were not very inconvenient, all this would be very
ludicrous.' The Colonial Office, at that moment a
branch of the Missionary Society, was deaf alike to
wisdom and loyalty, and thought it no shame to take
advantage of an unnamed, unrewarded talent. Though
politicians never mentioned him, Wakefield's part in
the mission to Canada was eminent, and acknowledged,
at least, by the chief himself. ' I have never erred,'
wrote Lord Durham, ' except when I rejected Wakefield's advice.' Where shall you find a nobler tribute
than that to unrecognised merit ? What part Wakefield had in the famous Durham report is unknown
and seems unknowable. ' Wakefield thought it ;
Buller wrote it ; Durham signed it.' Thus runs the
epigram, and perhaps its concision interferes not with
its truth.

Wakefield, meanwhile, never slackened his energy.
Invincible in toil, he wore himself out in the persuasion of his enemies and in the enlightenment of his
friends. Now it was the system of transportation
which engrossed him, an odious system which his
eloquence and determination brought to an end. Now
it was the Canterbury Settlement which demanded all
his courage and resource, and which more than any
enterprise quickened his generous enthusiasm. If he

were not a sound churchman, he was none the less an aristocrat in sympathy, and he saw in this exclusive colony a revival of the Elizabethan ideal.   Here at least there should be no meanness, and no plotting. All the colonists should be gentlemen, loyal to their Queen and their Church, while all the labourers should toil enthusiastically for the glory of the settlement.   But the demands of the Church were heavy, and one-third of the colony's capital was unproductive, so that its prosperity was doubtful for a while ; and had it not been for the faith of Wakefield, and the tactful energy of Godley, Canterbury would hardly have survived the opposition of Sir George Grey. However, the Pilgrims, as they called themselves, persevered, and once more Wakefield had reason to be proud of his experiment.

Meanwhile, the New Zealand Company had fallen upon evil days, and Wakefield, broken in health, was compelled to retire from its direction.   But he never lost confidence in the future, and it was with a good heart that he set sail—in 1853—to visit the colony over whose foundation he had watched so tenderly. He was now nearing sixty, and though he had devoted his whole life to our distant possessions, he knew them only by study and hearsay.   It was a strange confrontation between Wakefield and the colonists, whose prosperity had been assured by his energy and wisdom. And though Wakefield was enthusiastic in praise of the country, he never understood and never tolerated the narrow provincialism of the inhabitants.   He declared that no single New Zealander possessed so wide and general a knowledge of the place as himself, and he shrank in disgust from the envy which assailed him on all sides. 'There is an intense jealousy of new-comers,' he wrote, 'a state of feeling which always takes possession of young colonies, and holds them till they begin to be old.' Despite the common opposition, Wakefield threw himself into the politics of the place, was elected to the first Parliament of New Zealand, and speedily became the governor's confidential adviser. His opponents, in the end, were too strong for him : they cared not for his past services ; and, regarding him less as a benefactor than as a rival, they compelled his resignation. His active life was now at an end : rejected by the colony which with Lord Durham's aid he had created, he went into retirement, and died in 1862—neglected even by those whose prosperity he had assured.

His disastrous visit to New Zealand gives us a clue to Wakefield's talent. He never was and never could have been a practical colonist. He was a man of large ideas, who could devise a policy ; he could not fight the hard superstitions and pitiful jealousies of provincial vestrymen. He was a dreamer, a prophet, a clairvoyant, whose power of persuasion might always gain him the ear of other prophets and dreamers. His vivid temperament, his impatient enthusiasm, unfitted him for the dull routine of a colonial assembly. It was his business to make colonies, not to govern them, and so it came about that the New Zealanders scorned him when he came among them, and forgot him long before he was dead.

Now at last he is set upon the pedestal of honour, and we may contemplate impartially his character and achievement.   If his faults need any palliation at this day, palliation may be easily found.   So eagerly was he resolved to accomplish whatever end was in view, that he was not always too careful of the means.   Even when he carried off Miss Turner, he was influenced by the fact that she came from Macclesfield, and that after marriage he might have represented that place in the interest of the silk-weavers.   In another man so fantastic an excuse might have seemed hypocrisy. In Wakefield it was no hypocrisy, but merely a confession that in his brain the means and the end were inextricably mixed.   For the rest he was a simple, dignified gentleman, devoted to his daughter, whose death he never ceased to deplore, and always loyal to the call of friendship.   Sir Frederick Young pictures him as ' stout and burly in figure, with a smooth, round, fair face, looking very like a prosperous English farmer.'   He walked abroad accompanied by two talbot hounds ; and even when his counsel was most eagerly sought by statesmen, he lived a plain, secluded life, indignantly declining the patronage of the great.

His life is most deeply interesting, because it illustrates the real grandeur of England.   Whatever has been worthily achieved for our country has been achieved by private magnanimity.   The best of governments can do but little else than sanction the courage and patriotism of the adventurer. And it is because we have recognised this plain truth that we have colonised the world. France, with all her intelligence, has failed where we have succeeded. If she plants a province oversea, she too often perverts the experience she has gained at home. She insists on the supremacy of Paris, which knows no geography ; and she packs her colony so full with officials, government buildings, and restrictions, that little room is left for the enterprise of colonists.[1] We, on the other hand, leave our colonists free to find their own prosperity ; in the past we have either thwarted their courage or withheld our aid. But private energy has always triumphed over the lassitude of governments ; and if elsewhere the lassitude of governments is supreme, in England private energy is ultimately triumphant. And to this triumph no man has contributed more generously than Edward Gibbon Wakefield, who richly deserves whatever honour can be paid him. A tardy bust has been set up in the Colonial Office, but this is not enough ; and I can imagine no worthier monument to his memory than a fair reprint of the half-forgotten works, with the writing of which he expiated a crime and helped to found a colonial empire.

[1] The magnificent achievement of General Lyautey has proved that, with proper guidance, France need yield to none in the art of colonising.

BENJAMIN DISRAELI[1]

I.——BOYHOOD AND YOUTH

NO man of the nineteenth century had so keen a sense of adventure as Benjamin Disraeli. He had the rare faculty of colouring the smallest incidents of his life with the rainbow hues of fancy. That which to another might appear a trivial event seemed in his sanguine eyes a very miracle. His youth was a drama of hope and surprise. His happy temperament not merely made light of his misfortunes, which were neither few nor small, but persuaded him that his friends were the best in the world, his works the most brilliant, and the effect he was producing always irresistible. And the most precious of his gifts was his vitality. He lived with every sense and at every pore. Tireless in labour, tireless in pleasure, he easily achieved in the years of his splendid youth what the most of men would have spread over a long lifetime, and felt therein a proud contentment.

If the youth of Benjamin Disraeli was long and triumphant, his boyhood was brief indeed. In the common sense he never was a boy at all. His education was fragmentary and accidental. Of Jewish

---

[1] These pages on Disraeli were written as a comment upon Messrs. Monypenny and Buckle's *Life*, to which I am indebted for many quotations.

birth, he received his first serious lessons in the Academy of Mr. Potticany, an Independent minister, to whom succeeded as an instructor the Rev. Eli Cogan, an erudite Unitarian.[1] These are not the masters who might have been expected to train the mind of the young Disraeli, and it is not likely that he carried away from them many valuable lessons. The truth is, he took his own education in hand from the first, and preferred to indulge his genius as he chose. In the strict sense of the word he was never a scholar. Nevertheless, he made some progress in the study of the classics, and his youthful Diary proves that he read Lucian with interest, and Demosthenes with doubtful approval. His comments show that if he were not sensitive to the language, he was already a keen, if reckless, critic of oratory. Even at sixteen he had the wit to tear the meaning out of Greek, and to read the Greek authors as though they were living men. He is careless of grammar. It is characteristic of him that he speaks of ' Demosthenes' παρα του στεφανου.' It is characteristic also that at the age of sixteen, having bungled over the title of the speech, he is capable of the following tirade : ' I have a prejudice against Demosthenes, and though his speeches are replete with Virtue, Patriotism, and Courage, history tells me he was a Villain, a Partisan, and a Poltroon.'

[1] By a strange accident Disraeli's early education differed not from Bolingbroke's. Mr. Potticany and the Rev. Eli Cogan were to Disraeli what Daniel Burgess was to Bolingbroke. See above, p. 5.

To Disraeli his schooldays were not as they are to
the most of statesmen. It was not for him to pass
from Eton to Christ Church or Trinity, and to squeeze
his talents into the common mould. Not that a
formal education would have done him any harm.
His was the genius that would not in any case have
been profoundly affected by his environment. And
the immediate result of his training was that at an age
when boys of his own age were playing cricket he
was already a finished man of the world. A brief
sojourn in a lawyer's office did him neither ill nor
good. He was already determined upon enterprise,
and a first attempt to make a fortune by operating in
Spanish-American shares ended in disaster. 'What
concerns us,' says Mr. Monypenny, 'is that Disraeli
at the age of twenty had incurred a debt of several
thousand pounds—a debt which was not finally liqui-
dated till nearly thirty years later, when he had
already led the House of Commons and been Chancellor of the Exchequer.' His plight was grave, yet
not grave enough to dismay his courage. Already on
terms of friendship with John Murray, who had
consulted ' the precocious youth in the perplexities of
business,' Disraeli formed a magnificent project of
a Conservative newspaper which should preach a
sounder doctrine than *The Times*. *The Representative* it was to be called, and the story of its foundation, as told by Disraeli, both in his letters and in
Vivian Grey, is a brilliant piece of comedy. That
John Murray should have listened with enthusiasm

to Disraeli's project is a clear proof of the youth's confidence and persuasiveness. The terms were soon drawn up and duly signed. The property in the paper was ' to be vested as to one half in Murray, and as to the other half in equal shares in Powles [a solicitor] and Disraeli : the three contributed the capital in like proportions.' Of the obligation to provide his share, Disraeli's hopefulness no doubt made light. He saw only the chance of an adventure, which he was resolute to follow to the very end.

The story of his visit to Chiefswood has been often told. It will bear repetition. The first duty of the founders was to find a fitting editor for *The Representative*, and Murray's choice fell upon Lockhart. Nothing remained but to consult Sir Walter, and Disraeli was sent off to the north with two letters of introduction to Lockhart in his pocket, and a happy confidence in his heart. His journey was a kind of enchantment. Everything he saw by the way delighted him. He arrived at York in the midst of the Grand Festival ; he ' never witnessed a city in such an extreme bustle and so delightfully gay. It was a perfect carnival.' He was in the humour that admired everything. ' York Minster baffles all description. Westminster Abbey is a toy to it.' And the Minster was not the only thing that ravished his vision. ' I witnessed in York,' says he, ' another splendid sight—the pouring in of all the nobility and gentry of the neighbourhood and the neighbouring counties. The four-in-hands of the Yorkshire squires, the splendid rivalry in liveries and outriders, and the immense quantity of gorgeous equipages—numbers with four horses—formed a scene which you can only witness in the mighty and aristocratic county of York.' There speaks Disraeli with his own authentic voice. And even when the day was done he did not find the hours hang heavy on him. ' I find Froissart a most entertaining companion, just the fellow for a traveller's evening.'

His humour to admire ceased not at York. The earth could not hold a better place than Edinburgh. ' It is exactly what I fancied,' said he, ' and certainly is the most beautiful town in the world.' Lockhart was at Chiefswood, and thither Disraeli followed him. At the outset there was a disappointment. Lockhart, knowing nothing of the son, expected the father, and ' everything looked as black as possible.' Here was precisely the situation which the young Disraeli delighted to tackle. ' Suffice it to say,' he tells Murray, ' that in a few hours we completely understood each other, and were upon the most intimate terms. He [*i.e.* Lockhart] enters into our views with a facility and readiness which are capital. He thinks nothing can be more magnificent and excellent.' That there were difficulties in the way could not be denied. The Chevalier, as Disraeli, already in love with mystery, called Sir Walter, thought that Parliament for Lockhart was indispensable, and feared that the editorship of a daily paper was compromising to the dignity of a man of letters. Disraeli magniloquently explained

that the whole world was at their beck, and that
Lockhart would not be ' the Editor of a newspaper,
but the Director-General of an immense organ, and
at the head of a band of high-bred gentlemen and
important interests.'

Thus were the obstacles overcome. 'The young
coxcomb, a sprig of the root of Aaron,' as Sir Walter
described him, succeeded in making a vivid impression
both upon Sir Walter and upon the less impressionable
Lockhart, whom within three weeks he carried to
London, and whose agreement with Murray he duly
witnessed. In the calmer air of the metropolis there
was less talk of ' immense organs ' and ' Director-
Generals ' ; but Lockhart was installed as editor of
The Quarterly, and undertook ' to the best of his skill
and ability to aid and assist ' Murray in the pro-
duction of his newspaper, and ' by all means consistent with his rank in life ' to promote its sale and
character. So much the young Disraeli had achieved,
and his energy was by no means limited to the discovery
and appointment of an editor. He took offices,
arranged a printing place, engaged reporters and sub-
editors, appointed foreign correspondents, telling one
of them that the newspaper was to be ' the focus of the
information of the whole world,' and lightly assumed
the responsibility of the whole enterprise. ' Much,
my dear Lockhart,' he writes one day, ' has happened
since we parted, I think, of importance. In the first
place, *Maginn is engaged*.' His description of this
crowning exploit is like a page out of one of his novels.

When Disraeli had unfolded his scheme ' the Doctor started from his chair like Giovanni in the banquet scene, and seemed as astounded—as *attonitus*—as Porsenna when Scævola missed him. A new world seemed open to him, and this sneering scribe, this man of vast experience, who had so smiled at our first mentioning the business, ended by saying that as to the success of the affair doubt could not exist, and that a year could not elapse without our being the first paper going. . . . In brief, the Doctor goes to Paris.'

From the first it seemed an unequal combat. On the one side was youth and life and faith, which laughed at difficulties. On the other were experience, distrust, and intrigue, which knew well how to invent stumbling-blocks. Murray took fright at Croker's opposition to Lockhart, and sent Disraeli to Scotland once more that he might persuade Sir Walter to write to his friends in London. Sir Walter did what he could, and ' administered a dose of physic ' to Murray as well. In due course the ill-fated newspaper, *The Representative*, made its appearance under the title selected by Disraeli, lingered infirm and undistinguished for a few months, and then died of inanition. For its career Disraeli was in no sense to blame. He had disappeared from the councils of Lockhart and Murray some weeks before the first number was printed. Perhaps he was submerged in the financial panic which smote London towards the end of 1826. Whatever the cause, he withdrew suddenly from the enterprise, in whose inception he had played the largest part, and incurred the lasting resentment of John Murray. Whether this resentment was due to any action of Disraeli's or to the suspicion that Murray was caricatured in *Vivian Grey* cannot now be determined. At least it must be said that the failure of *The Representative* was in no sense discreditable to Disraeli, and if in after years he did not care to recall the episode, it was because the mind of man dwells with the greatest satisfaction upon the memory of success. As Mr. Monypenny truly says, ' he had shown amazing energy, amazing self-confidence, and amazing power of winning to his views men older and riper in experience than himself. His faults had been the faults of youth, an over-sanguine temperament, and immaturity of judgment.' Who knows but that, had he remained to stimulate Murray and Lockhart with his courage and high spirits, *The Representative* might have achieved a splendid triumph ?

Bitter as instant failure always is, the episode of Murray's newspaper was by no means unprofitable to Disraeli. Not merely did it give him excellent material for his first romance ; it taught him the lesson, learned in misfortune by Contarini Fleming, that imagination will always get the worst of it in a tussle with experience. It was more valuable to Disraeli than it might have been to another, because nothing was lost to his apprehensive brain. His early years were spent sedulously in the making of himself. It was as though he knew precisely the character and temperament which he meant to mould, as though he

neglected nothing in the fashioning of the man who
would one day stand before the world as Benjamin
Disraeli. *The Representative* pointed out the path
which the man of affairs must take. His famous
journey to the East quickened his fancy, and showed
him how the stern realities of foreign policy might be
coloured by romance. Before he set forth, like
another Bacchus, to conquer the Orient, he was
destined to traverse an arid desert of despondency.
It was as though two years had been blotted from his
life. He himself was perfectly conscious of disaster.
' I am at present quite idle,' he wrote to Sharon Turner,
' being at this moment slowly recovering from one of
those tremendous disorganisations which happen to
all men at some period of their lives, and which are
perhaps equally necessary for the formation of both
body and constitution.' With his rapid intelligence
Disraeli discovered good in the evil, and went forth
to seek health with a high courage. That he should
turn his face eastwards was natural enough. He
believed devoutly that ' all is race,' and piety persuaded
him to travel towards the rising sun in search of the
cradle of his tribe. Moreover, the influence of Byron
was at its height, and Byronism was in the very blood
of Disraeli. Thus everything conspired to make this
journey to the East the turning-point of his career.
Disraeli wrote nothing afterwards that was not touched
by its influence. There is no doubt whatever that
the Eastern questions, to which he devoted so much of
his thought and policy, would have found a very

different solution had not Disraeli set out with Meredith in 1830 to see the world.

The admirable letters, in which he described his travels, were published long since. Familiarity cannot stale them. They are as fresh and vivid to-day as on the day when they were written. An immortal gaiety informs them. Every line bears the impress of self-satisfaction. The author takes it for granted that to him at least the last excess of coxcombry is permitted. At Gibraltar he had 'the fame of being the first who ever passed the Straits with two canes, a morning and an evening cane. I change my cane as the gun fires, and hope to carry them both on to Cairo. It is wonderful the effect these magical wands produce. I owe to them even more attention than to being the supposed author of—what is it ? I forget ! ' As he went farther from home, his nonchalance increased. He found in Clay, who had joined his party, an excellent foil. 'To govern men,' he wrote from Malta, ' you must either excel them in their accomplishments or despise them. Clay does the one, I do the other, and we are both equally popular. Affectation tells here even better than wit. Yesterday at the racket-court, sitting in the gallery among strangers, the ball entered and lightly struck me and fell at my feet. I picked it up, and observing a young rifleman excessively stiff, I humbly requested him to forward its passage into the court, as I had really never thrown a ball in my life. This incident has been the general subject of conversation at all the messes to-day.'

In this incident there is the real touch of Disraeli.
It is easy to believe that all the messes discussed the
traveller's lackadaisical ignorance of sport. It is
unlikely that their comments would have pleased him.
It is rumoured, indeed, that his coxcombry made him
intolerable at Malta, and that the Officers' Mess,
delighted with Clay's society, ceased to invite ' that
damned bumptious Jew boy.' If that were true, it
made no difference to Disraeli's demeanour. He
always assumed an indifference to the opinions of
others, and in 1830 at any rate he cannot have been
very sensitive to ridicule. His love of extravagant
costume already overpowered him. It was as though
he were always dressing-up for some fantastic charade.
All the extravagance of the East was in the fashions
that he cultivated, and he was charmed with the
curiosity of the vulgar. To be pointed at—*mon-
starier hic est*—was an experience novel enough to be
delightful, and he was honest enough to brag of his
buffooneries.

He dined one day at a regimental dinner dressed
as an Andalusian. Meredith tells us that he paid
a round of visits ' in his majo jacket, white trousers,
and a sash of all the colours of the rainbow ; in
this wonderful costume he paraded all round Valetta,
followed by one-half the population of the place,
and, as he said, putting a complete stop to all
business.' This last exploit must have brought real
joy to his ambitious heart, and we need not puzzle our
minds whether he was careless or unconscious of the

effect he produced. At any rate he brazened it out finely. ' You should see me in the costume of a Greek pirate,' he writes to his brother from Malta. ' A blood-red shirt, with silver studs as big as shillings, an immense scarf for girdle, full of pistols and daggers, red cap, red slippers, broad blue-striped jacket and trousers.' It is amazing, and none can be surprised that the *militaires*, as he calls them, disapproved of his antics. He took an appropriate revenge. ' By heavens ! ' he said, ' I believe these fellows are boys till they are Majors, and sometimes do not even stop there.' Yet none of them had the supreme boyishness of their critic, who cheerfully faced the world in blood-red shirt and blue trousers.

The farther East he went the more daringly was he compelled to claim the attention of others. ' The rich and various costumes of the Levant ' tempted him to the last magnificence. When he was presented to the Grand Vizier he ransacked his ' heterogeneous wardrobe ' to contrive such a costume as should astound that august personage. ' I am quite a Turk,' he wrote from Yanina, ' wear a turban, smoke a pipe six feet long, and squat on a divan. Mehemet Pasha told me that he did not think I was an Englishman, because I walked so slow ; in fact, I find the habits of this calm and luxurious people entirely agree with my own preconceived opinions of propriety and enjoyment, and I detest the Greeks more thàn ever.' Thus we find him carousing with a Bey at Previsa, and exulting in his amicable reception by Ali Pasha, in whose Hall of Audience he seated himself on the divan of the Grand Vizier 'with the self-possession of a morning call.' It was at Constantinople that he reached the climax of his journey. 'It is near sunset,' he wrote, 'and Constantinople is in full sight ; it baffles all description, though so often described. An immense mass of buildings, cupolas, cypress groves, and minarets. I feel an excitement which I thought was dead.'

The last sentence is, of course, a hint of the familiar pose. In Disraeli's heart and brain enthusiasm never died. He lived in a white heat, which fused with his soul the experience of the moment. As I have said, his journey to the East profoundly influenced his word and deed. When he came back his nature had undergone (so to say) a chemical change. He had visited his origins, and found in Judaism a solution of the problems of the West. Like Contarini he turned the tables on 'the flat-nosed Franks,' and exulted henceforth in the temper of his Eastern home. But as from the first it was his ambition to serve England, he recognised that a knowledge of Englishmen was necessary to his development. And so he made a brilliant entry into Society, which, as he knew well, held in its hand the key of political preferment. Again, it seems as though he were consciously moulding his own life and character ; and if in all that he does there is a certain purpose, that purpose in no sense diminishes Disraeli's frank delight in his success. Many were the advantages which he brought to the conquest of

London. He was handsome, witty, and debonair. Accustomed from his childhood to mix with scholars, he had tempered his learning in the fire of the Orient, and he carried into what he would call ' the *salons* of the great' a separate knowledge of life and words. He met many who knew more than he did. He met none who knew precisely the same things, and thus it was that his niche was ready to receive him.

Moreover, he could talk brilliantly when he chose. A still rarer accomplishment was his, he could be silent. He understood the light and shade of conversation, and never made himself tiresome or ridiculous by a too insistent volubility. When Mrs. Wyndham Lewis told him that she liked ' silent, melancholy men,' she was but flattering his pride. Moreover, the habit of masquerade, which he had cultivated in the East, had not left him. Whether Society liked him or not, Society could not ignore a man who came before it so oddly suited. His apparel long since became a legend, and seems, in these days of uniformity, an outrage upon taste and tact. If any one dared to present himself before the world to-day in the fantastic disguises which Disraeli affected, he would be driven into retirement with insult. It must be remembered, of course, that Disraeli lived in a fantastic age. Even D'Orsay, the master of fashion, the supreme arbiter of elegancies, permitted himself a freedom of manner and attire which would have shocked the dandies. And Disraeli surpassed D'Orsay in extravagance far more than D'Orsay surpassed the

exquisites of the Regency.   It was Brummel's laudable
ambition to walk down St. James's Street unnoticed.
It was Disraeli's purpose to be noticed before all others
wherever he went.   In brief, he assumed a sort of
fancy dress as a short cut to fame, and hoped by this
means to atone for the absence of family connections
and conventional education.

That he went no further in masquerade than the
necessities of the case demanded we can easily believe.
He knew his public, and though his taste was ever
flamboyant, he was an artist in life as in other things.
And if we may believe his contemporaries, he was a
kind of Osric, a veritable water-fly.   Here is Lady
Dufferin's description of him : ' He wore a black
velvet coat lined with satin, purple trousers with a
gold band running down the outside seam, a scarlet
waist-coat, long lace ruffles falling down to the tips of
his fingers, and long black ringlets rippling down upon
his shoulders.'   Even on the hustings he did not
mitigate his fancy.   He appeared at Taunton ' very
showily attired in a dark bottle-green frock-coat, a
waist-coat of the most extravagant pattern, the front
of which was almost covered with glittering chains,
and in fancy-pattern pantaloons.   He wore a plain
black stock, but no collar was visible.   Altogether,'
says a spectator, ' he was the most intellectual-looking
exquisite I had ever seen.'   That such antics should
have acquired notoriety for him is not surprising.
That they should not in the slightest degree have
diminished the respect in which he was held by his

friends is the highest tribute to his worth and power
of fascination.

Such were some of the guises in which he conquered
London, and every step in his triumphal progress is
recorded in the letters which he wrote home. ' I wish,'
wrote his father, ' that your organisation allowed you
to write calmer letters.' The wish was vain. Disraeli's
enthusiasm broke down every barrier of restraint.
He lived always on the top of the wave. For him
the Ocean of Society was ever buoyant and sparkling
in the sunshine. He knew only the ' first-rate '
people, and welcomed with pride the dislike of the
second-rate   One night there is a ' brilliant *réunion* '
at Bulwer's, with Strangford, Mulgrave, and D'Orsay
among the notables ; another day he sits at dinner
between Peel and Herries. A few months later he is
living upon terms of friendship with the incomparable
Mrs. Norton, and her sister, Mrs. Blackwood, ' also
very handsome and very Sheridanic.' His table is
' literally covered with invitations,' many from people
whom he does not know. ' I have passed the whole
of this year in uninterrupted lounging and pleasure,'
he confides to his Diary in September 1833. Then
he became very popular with the dandies, and the
crown was set upon his social career. ' D'Orsay took
a fancy to me,' he writes, ' and they take their tune
from him. Lady Blessington is their muse, and she
declared violently in my favour.' Thus it was that
all the houses in England opened their doors to him,
and when he came before the world as a politician few

men were better known to their contemporaries than
Disraeli the Younger.

Of Disraeli's novels I shall have something to say
presently.   It is easy to dispraise the fantastic extravagance of *Vivian Grey*, *The Young Duke*, and the rest.
They are as gaily unbridled as their author's costume.
They are all untrammelled by the restraints of grammar
and common-sense.   But these faults are not organic.
They do not diminish in any way the abounding
vitality of Disraeli's early romances.   The first part
of *Vivian Grey* is a masterpiece of art and energy.
That the rest falls below it in interest—is in fact
almost unreadable—casts no shadow on a brilliant
sketch.   It reminds us only that Disraeli could not
always sustain his inspiration unto the end of a book.
There is not one of these early works—except,
perhaps, *Venetia*—which shows no sign of weariness.
You cannot open them at random without happening
upon a brilliant phrase, a flash of wit, or a piece of swift
insight into the springs of human action.   And the
publication of his early books gave Disraeli that
appreciation abroad which he always coveted.

Mr. Monypenny, for instance, quotes Heine's tribute
to the excellences of *Contarini Fleming*, and the criticism of one Jew by another is worth remembering.
'Modern English letters,' says Heine, 'have given us
no offspring equal to *Contarini Fleming*.   Cast in
the Teutonic mould, it is nevertheless one of the most
original works ever written : profound, poignant,
pathetic ; its subject the most interesting, if not the

noblest, imaginable—the development of a poet ; truly
psychological ; passion and mockery ; Gothic rude-
ness, the fantasy of the Saracens, and yet over all a
classic, even a death-like, repose.' This is high praise
indeed, which, with Goethe's admiration of *Vivian
Grey*, might have satisfied even one so hungry for
flattery as Benjamin Disraeli. In *Contarini Fleming*
the author still kept an eye upon his own character.
He was not merely writing a novel ; he was clarify-
ing his ideas and shaping his own career as well as
Contarini's. In *Venetia* he suppresses himself utterly,
and is content to draw with the finest tact and sympathy the portraits of Byron and Shelley. The book
shows a power of understanding and criticising others
which Disraeli had not hitherto exhibited, and it is
impossible to praise too highly his just intuition.

These early novels of Disraeli's belong to the
Romantic Movement which, as he grew to manhood,
held Europe in its grip. Born in England of Gray's
Odes and Percy's *Reliques*, encouraged by Scott and
Byron, it was destined to produce its greatest effect in
France. But it is characteristic of Disraeli that he
owed nothing to the famous *Romantiques*. Byron
was the source of his romance, as he was one of their
sources also ; and we find Disraeli writing to Lady
Blessington in 1834 for information concerning the
novelists of France. ' What do you think of the
modern French novelists,' he asks, ' and is it worth my
while to read them, and if so, what do you recommend ?
What of Balzac,—is he better than Sue and Geo.

Sand Dudevant, and are those inferior to Hugo ?
I ask you these questions because you will give me
short answers, like all people who are masters of their
subject.' We know not Lady Blessington's answer,
and we are left wondering what influence the courage
and grandeur of Balzac would have had upon the mind
of Disraeli. Would Disraeli, like Thackeray, have
perversely misunderstood the master ? Or would he,
with the example of the *Comédie Humaine* before him,
have made a resolute attempt to discover the truth
of common things ? We are not sanguine. Disraeli's
temperament was too strong, too intimately his
own, to surrender to another's genius, and I fear that
the *Mysteries of Paris* would have been more easily
intelligible to him.than *Cousine Bette*.

Disraeli, as I have said, was the real hero of his own
romances. His life and his novels are inextricably
bound up together. Of this close relationship he
makes full confession. ' My works,' he writes, ' are
the embodification of my feelings. In *Vivian Grey* I
have portrayed my active and real ambition ; in *Alroy*
my ideal ambition ; *The Psychological Romance* is a
development of my poetic character. This trilogy
is the secret history of my feelings. I shall write
no more about myself.' Though he did not keep his
word, though he was destined to write much more
about himself, the statement that his works embody his
feelings is true enough. The conflict, especially,
which Contarini witnessed in his mind between active
ambition and poetic creation, was witnessed also by

the introspective eye of Disraeli. The result was not
long in doubt. ' Poetry,' said he, ' is the safety-valve
of my passions, but I wish to act what I write.' This
wish to act grew stronger with the years. Literary
expression became more and more a mere means of
satisfying exigent creditors. The necessity of doing
something was soon imperative. ' I am never well,'
he tells Lady Blessington at last, ' save in action, and
then I am immortal.' When once he had realised
this truth he could hesitate no longer. He was in his
own eyes a man of destiny, and he saw plainly where
his destiny lay. Henceforth literature must be
subordinate to his real ambition, which was to govern
men. Politics must be his means, statesmanship his
goal ; and he entered upon his new career with all
his zest and courage.

From the very first he had perfect faith in himself.
Even in the time of his illness and despondency his
confidence did not desert him. ' There is something
within me,' he wrote, ' which, in spite of all the dicta
of the faculty and in the face of the prostrate state in
which I lie, whispers to me that I shall yet weather
this fearful storm, and that a more prosperous career
may yet open to me.' There breathes the very spirit
of conquest, and when he was definitely resolved to go
in for politics he had but to make up his mind on which
side his sympathies were engaged. His ambition was
definite. When Lord Melbourne asked him what his
object might be, he answered without hesitation, ' To
be Prime Minister ' ; and Lord Melbourne lived long

enough to confess, ' By God ! the fellow will do it yet.' And he meant to achieve his ambition by his own energies. He knew that he must fight his own battle, and that until he had won at least one round, nobody would help him. When he was asked upon what he stood, he replied, ' On my head,' and never was a truer answer given. But, as I have said, he was uncertain on which side to range himself. He was, of course, a natural Tory, if as yet he knew it not. He had expressed something of his wavering uncertainty in *The Young Duke*. ' Am I a Whig or a Tory ? ' he asked. ' I forget. As for the Tories, I admire antiquity, and particularly a ruin ; even the relics of the Temple of Intolerance have a charm. I think I am a Tory. But then the Whigs give such good dinners and are the most amusing ; I think I am a Whig. But then the Tories are so moral, and morality is my forte ; I must be a Tory. But the Whigs dress so much better ; and an ill-dressed party, like an ill-dressed man, must be wrong. Yes, I am a decided Whig. And yet—I feel like Garrick between Tragedy and Comedy.' It is excellent fooling. But Disraeli did not long share the Young Duke's uncertainty. If he did not at once declare himself a Tory, he lost little time in anathematising the Whigs.

When he stood first for High Wycombe his position was clear enough. ' I start in the high Radical interest,' he said, ' and take down strong recommendatory epistles from O'Connell, Hume, Burdett, and *hoc genus.* Toryism is worn out, and I cannot condescend to be a Whig.' Standing firmly upon that platform, he showed at once his great oratorical gifts. ' I jumped up on the portico of the Red Lion,' he wrote, ' and gave it them for an hour and a quarter. I can give you no idea of the effect. I made them all mad. A great many absolutely cried.' But either the enthusiasts were not voters, or they did not vote for him. He was beaten at the poll, and instantly prepared for another contest. In all his speeches he struck with great effect the same note of hatred of the Whigs. ' Rid yourselves of all that political jargon and fatuous slang of Whig and Tory,' he tells his constituents,—' two names with one meaning, used only to delude you ; and unite in forming a great national party, which alone can save the country from impending destruction.' Thus he appealed against the Whigs to Sir William Windham and my Lord Bolingbroke, and at each appearance drew nearer and nearer to the Tories. At Aylesbury he stood on the hustings as the supporter of the second Tory candidate, and he did not a little in these first contests to bring the Tories and the Radicals together,—not such a hopeless task as it might seem. In less than two years his allegiance to Toryism was openly pronounced. Meantime he had met Lord Lyndhurst, who believed that the end of Whiggism was at hand, and who was ' looking about for a party to put in motion which might not seem factious.' Disraeli, who, though determined upon a political career, had then no political relations, eagerly joined forces with Lyndhurst, and friends and allies they remained until the end.

Henceforth Disraeli's path was clearly marked. A few months later he was nominated for the Carlton Club, and became an acknowledged and official member of the Tory party. Unfortunately he had already given hostages to fortune on the other side, and had exposed himself openly to the attacks of his enemies. When he went as a candidate to Taunton, D'Orsay, the best of friends and the wisest of counsellors, told him that it was absolutely essential for him to explain ' that though a Tory he was a reforming one ; because it was generally understood that he had committed himself in some degree with the other party.' Disraeli took the advice after his own fashion. He told his electors that if there was anything upon which he piqued himself, it was on his consistency. ' Gentlemen,' said he, ' here is my consistency. I have always opposed with my utmost energy the party of which my honourable opponent is a distinguished member. That party I have opposed for reasons I am prepared to give and to uphold. I look upon the Whigs as the anti-National party.' This explanation is perfectly just. Disraeli had always, even in the early days of Wycombe, supported the cause of England against the domination of the Whig tenants for life. But the charge of inconsistency, once made, stuck to Disraeli like a burr, and not for many a long year did he overcome the venial indiscretion of 1832.

Consistency is the very meanest of the virtues. It is not worth the while of any serious statesman to pique himself upon it. It happens by a strange irony that Disraeli can lay a sounder claim to consistency than almost any other ruler. Mr. Monypenny puts the matter clearly enough. ' It is no accident,' he says, ' that there is a certain ambiguity about the party affiliations of nearly all our greater statesmen : Chatham, Pitt, Burke, Canning, Peel, Palmerston, Disraeli, and Gladstone—none of these has an absolutely consistent party record ; and indeed a man with such a record would be more likely to win distinction as a good partisan than as a statesman. If we are to measure consistency by ideas, Disraeli is the most consistent of them all, and yet more than any of the others he was to suffer throughout his career from the reputation of political time-server and adventurer.'

Why was this ? In the first place, I think, because the scurrilous attacks of O'Connell and Disraeli's energetic treatment of that demagogue called the whole world's attention to Disraeli's change of view. And then the charge of adventure and inconsistency was an easy charge for Disraeli's many opponents to bring. That he should have had opponents was essential to his career and the natural result of his character. There was something provocative in his attitude and demeanour. He was in those early days a fighter, who gave no quarter and expected none. Of course he was no more an adventurer than any other young man of gentle birth and good breeding who essays to make a name for himself in politics. But he did not come of one of the great families. He dared to put a new construction upon old principles, to vivify the dead bones of controversy, to skip the centuries and to go back for guidance to Bolingbroke. And so he made enemies with his bitter tongue and his quick intellect, and his enemies found no retort more ready to their hand than the taunts of inconsistency and adventure.

However, at last Disraeli is coming into his kingdom. The man who neither 'complained nor explained' is better understood to-day than ever he was. To justify Disraeli's conduct, to appreciate his genius, nothing is necessary save knowledge, and an end has at last been put for ever to the injurious legends which have gathered about his name. That he was an honourable gentleman, in spite of the web of debt in which he was caught while still a boy, the wise have always believed. It is now certain. The pose, which exasperated the foolish, was the pose of perfect sincerity. Disraeli fashioned himself, as he thought he should be fashioned, with the same detachment wherewith he fashioned his works of literary art. His candour was absolute. He made no secret of his qualities either to himself or others. It was wholly impossible for him to do or say anything unconsciously. If he seemed a mystery, as he hoped, it was because a triple brass of self-consciousness involved him : never was he taken off his guard ; seldom did he descend to the natural or expected deed or word. For all that he was, as I have said, a model of sincerity. Not merely was he consistent with himself ; he was consistent with his works, whose irony and cynicism were part of his own nature. His devotion to his family, his aptitude for friendship—what young man ever had stauncher friends than D'Orsay and Lyndhurst ?—are another eloquent tribute to his character. Such was the man who, confident in his own gifts, entered Parliament in 1837 as member for Maidstone, and grew at last into the statesman who played a gallant part amid the clash of parties, in what he himself was wont to call the Senate.

II.—IN PARLIAMENT

If Disraeli's career, after he had entered Parliament, lost something in the high spirits of adventurous youth, it gained much in a grave consistency of purpose. In 1837, Disraeli had sowed the wild oats of fancy, and none knew more confidently than he that the seeds of a wanton extravagance were to bring forth a rich harvest of political achievement. He had gained by a brilliant and deliberate eccentricity the goal of social success. And henceforth, until the end of his life, his eyes were fixed firmly upon the House of Commons. As member for Maidstone, as the colleague of Mr. Wyndham Lewis, he claimed and won a consideration which did not belong to the bold candidate still wavering between a reckless Radicalism and the philosophic Toryism of Bolingbroke. But though the years of romance were finished, Disraeli still cherished an inveterate habit of optimism. Though the battle was by no means over, he saw himself always in the centre of the field, an easy victor. The demon of doubt never whispered a paralysing syllable in his ear. His home-letters still burn with a fiery confidence. He is conscious that all eyes are upon him. He knows that he is singled out for particular favours. ' The dinner to-day,' says he, when as a member he is but a day old, ' is merely a House dinner of fourteen—all our great men with the exception of Lord Ramsay and myself, the only two new members. It has occasioned some jealousy and surprise.' If it was Disraeli's first Parliament, it was Queen Victoria's first Parliament also, and to the general wonder there was a division on the Address. It took an hour, and Disraeli entered into it with all the zest of a novice. ' I left the House at ten o'clock,' thus he writes, ' none of us having dined. The tumult and excitement great. I dined, or rather supped, at the Carlton with a large party off oysters, Guinness, and broiled bones, and got to bed at half-past twelve o'clock. Thus ended the most remarkable day hitherto of my life.'

The enthusiasm is characteristic. He found every day remarkable, and the last the most remarkable of them all. He took up politics, as he took up Society, with a light heart and an iron hand, and his triumph was ensured. It was not the least of his good fortune that his maiden speech, delivered on 7th December 1837, should have been received with an unparalleled demonstration of hostility. The occasion long ago claimed the place in history which it will never surrender. It was an Irish debate, and Disraeli deliberately elected to follow O'Connell, his ancient enemy. 'We shall meet again at Philippi '—this had been his challenge, and at Philippi they stood face to face. He attacked his ancient enemy in the admirable phrases of which he was master. O'Connell's speech was 'a rhetorical medley.' O'Connell's subscription was 'a project of majestic mendicancy.' If Disraeli's dandyism lost him the sympathy of many even in his own party, his spirited attack upon O'Connell roused a storm of fury among the Irish. 'Hisses, groans, hoots, cat-calls, drumming with the feet, loud conversation, and imitation of animals,' we are told, greeted every one of his sallies. Throughout it all he remained unperturbed. Not for one moment was his temper ruffled. Whenever there was an interlude of silence he spoke another period of his prepared speech in a cold, even, relentless voice. He twitted the noble Tityrus of the Treasury Bench and the learned Daphnis of Liskeard, and he painted a famous picture of Lord John Russell 'from his pedestal of power wielding in one hand the keys of St. Peter and waving with the other——' The sentence was never completed, but Disraeli was not slow to inform his friends that had he been allowed to proceed he would have put in the noble lord's other hand the cap of liberty. Thus, amid an unexampled uproar, he drew on to his memorable peroration : ' I sit down now, but the time will come when you will hear me.'

Henceforth Disraeli's place in the House was assured. A respectable speech, delivered and heard in silence, might have been his undoing. The hostility of the Irish had assured him a brilliant effect. Henceforth he was familiar to every gossip in the kingdom as the man who had been shouted down and had not winced at the punishment. For a moment, it is true, even his own serener confidence was shaken, but for a moment only. A breath of encouragement speedily blew away the cobwebs of his doubt. Chandos congratulated him in the lobby. ' I replied,' writes he to his sister, ' that I thought there was no cause for congratulations, and muttered "Failure !" "No such thing," said Chandos ; "you are quite wrong. I have just seen Peel, and I said to him, ' Now, tell me exactly what you think of D." Peel replied, ' Some of my party are disappointed and talk of failure. I say *just the reverse*. He did all that he could do under the circumstances. I say anything but failure ; he must make his way.' " '

Where Peel led, the others followed. Lyndhurst made light of the bullying of the Radicals. He was sure that Disraeli ' would have the courage to have at them again.' But the man whose eulogy most warmly gratified the orator was Sheil. ' Now, gentlemen,' said Sheil in Bulwer's hearing, ' I have heard all you have to say, and, what is more, I heard

this same speech of Mr. Disraeli, and I tell you this :
if ever the spirit of oratory was in a man, it is in that
man.   Nothing can prevent him being one of the
first speakers in the House of Commons [great
confusion].   Ay ! I know something about that
place, I think, and I tell you what besides, that if there
had not been this interruption, Mr. Disraeli might
have made a failure.   I don't call this a failure, it is
a crush.   My *début* was a failure, because I was
heard, but my reception was supercilious, his malignant.   A *début* should be dull.   The House will not
allow a man to be a wit and an orator unless they have
the credit of finding it out.'   It was a generous
appreciation, which led to a friendship and much good
counsel.   Sheil, a master of Parliamentary tactics, not
only praised Disraeli, he advised him : ' Get rid of
your genius for a session,' said he. . . . ' Speak often,
for you must not show yourself cowed, but speak
shortly. . . . Quote figures, dates, calculations.   And
in a short time the House will sigh for the wit and
eloquence which they all know are in you.'   Never
was better advice given, nor more wisely received.
The next time Disraeli spoke in the House he was
careful to be dull.

As I have said, among the many reproaches hurled
at Disraeli at the outset of his career was the charge
of political tergiversation.   He was still denounced
for a renegade on a hundred platforms.   His early
adventures in the cause of Radicalism were recalled
to his mind with a pompous iteration.   Yet Disraeli

was more sternly uniform than any of his colleagues or rivals.   From the doctrine of Tory Democracy he never wavered.   If he had found his formula in the eighteenth century, he had stuck to it and made it his own.   He was unalterable in his opposition to the Whiggish oligarchy.   He fought the selfishness of the greedy middle-class with all the weapons of his forensic eloquence.   ' I look upon the Whigs as the anti-National party,' he had said on the hustings at Taunton, and he repeated the phrase with variations again and again.   In 1840 he assured Charles Attwood that he had worked for no other object and no other end than to aid the formation of a national party.   ' I entirely agree with you,' he wrote, ' that an union between the Conservative Party and the Radical masses offers the only means by which we can preserve the Empire.'

And the consistency of Disraeli came from no desire to entrench himself against attack.   He was consistent, because before all things he was a political philosopher.   For him the division bell was not the one and only excuse of statesmanship.   He accepted the House of Commons, with its rules of procedure and its passion of parties, as a convenient method of government.   None more loyally than he respected its traditions and guarded its privileges.   But he was a statesman of fixed principles, which he would if he could persuade the House to carry out.   The last lines of *Sybil* have been quoted many times.   They cannot be quoted too often, for they contain in a small space the essence of the Disraelian doctrine.   ' That

we may live to see England once more possess a free
Monarchy, and a privileged and prosperous People,
is my prayer ; that these great consequences can only
be brought about by the energy and devotion of our
Youth is my persuasion.   We live in an age when
to be young and to be indifferent can be no longer
synonymous.   We must prepare for the coming
hour.   The claims of the Future are represented by
suffering millions ; and the Youth of a Nation are the
trustees of Posterity.'

With this faith emblazoned on his banner Disraeli
went forth to fight.   It inspired him not only in the
battle of Young England but in his fierce contest with
Peel.   Each of these episodes was a necessary step in
Disraeli's progress.   They won him the two things
of which he stood urgently in need—Parliamentary
fame and the support of the aristocracy.   The good
fortune which seldom deserts the adventurous spirit
perched happily upon Disraeli's shoulder.   The brief
glory of Young England, if it attained no definite
object, was Disraeli's first real triumph in the House.
It strengthened his position ; it crystallised his views.
That he should have taken the lead of the generous
spirits who had come down from Cambridge, eager
to reform the world, was natural.   Disraeli always
professed a keen sympathy with men younger than
himself.   He had a profound belief in the efficacy of
youth.   Before Young England could claim to be a
party, he was already on terms of intimacy with Lord
John Manners and George Smythe, the apostles of the

new gospel. ' I find myself without effort the leader of a party,' he wrote to his wife as early as March 1842, ' chiefly of the youth and new members. Lord John Manners came to me about a motion which he wanted me to bring forward, and he would second it like Claud Hamilton. Henry Baillie the same about Afghanistan. I find my position changed.' Nor was it strange that Lord John Manners and Smythe should willingly seek the guidance of Disraeli. He was a man of ardour, equal with their own, and of far wider experience. A yet stronger bond between them was a community of thought and interest. The doctrine of Tory Democracy, which Disraeli expounded with so brilliant an effect, had been evolved by them at Eton and Cambridge, in complete independence and sincerity. And when, new to Parliament, they heard Disraeli pleading the cause of the people, they hailed him with enthusiasm as the leader of their party.

Young England, as we discern it in retrospect, was a clear outcome of the Romantic Movement. Literary in its origin and inspiration, it made a valiant attempt to turn the light of imagination upon the dark places of politics. George Smythe and Lord John Manners, its only begetters, were poets by temperament, politicians by training and ambition. But above all they were true Romantics. For them the age of chivalry was not dead. The influences of their childhood and their youth were feudal and Byronic. To feudalism they were born ; the lessons of Byronism they had learned at school and college, and had

given to them the ampler interpretation of magnani-
mous youth.   Moreover, they had read the Waverley
Novels with passion, and rejoiced in the popular love
of antiquities.   They were fervent legitimists both ;
they still cherished the sentiment of the Jacobites ;
and Lord John Manners had proved in Spain a practical
sympathy with the Carlists.   A meeting with
F. W. Faber at the Lakes had inclined them both to
the doctrines of the High Church party, and they were
near enough to the Oxford Movement, another off-
shoot of Romance, to fall beneath the spell of Newman.
Clearly for them a Whig alliance was impossible.
They came forward as the champions of the monarchy
and the people.   ' O for an hour of George Canning ! '
exclaimed George Smythe on a famous occasion, and
the admirers of Canning could not but be as hostile to
Peel as to the Whigs themselves.

Mr. Monypenny explains their political views with
justice and lucidity.   ' They devised for the Church,'
says he, ' a position of greater independence than the
Erastian spirit of the eighteenth century had been
willing to sanction, or that Peel himself, we may
surmise, would have been disposed to concede.   Like
all true Romantics, they had an antipathy to the
middle-class, which was Peel's political idol : they
dreaded its growing influence, and hoped to provide
a counterpoise by rewakening the sense of duty in the
nobility and gentry, and restoring them to their right-
ful place as leaders and protectors of the people.   With
the people at large their sympathy was real and active.

They had that faith in the lower orders which the Tory party had lost, and the courage to believe that it might be possible to redeem them from the misery and serfdom into which they had fallen. Their minds were fertile in ideas, some of them too picturesque, perhaps, to be practical, but all of them noble and disinterested, for bringing back joy to the sombre and monotonous lives of the labouring poor, and renewing the harmony between classes that had been one of the characteristics of the " Merrie England " of the past.' It was a lofty and a noble aspiration, and that Young England failed is the worst misfortune that could have fallen upon the people. Unhappily democracy has taken the road of serfdom, and to-day we see a vision which would have pitifully distressed the champions of 1842, a vision of working men enslaved by their own leaders and by the mischievous men they have put in office—enslaved and with no other freedom than a vote.

Such were the views of Young England, and worthily were they advocated by the youthful heroes who composed the party. Of these, as we have said, the most conspicuous were Lord John Manners and George Smythe. Lord John was, as Mr. Monypenny well says, ' a man of a loyalty, purity, and kindliness of nature that almost amounted to genius.' Other gifts were his also. He had a natural talent for politics, and grew with the years into a keen debater and a wise administrator. The advocacy of the people's cause was his peculiar contribution to Young England's

stock of ideas.   Disraeli drew him with a discerning
hand as Lord Henry Sydney in *Coningsby*.   ' An
indefinite yet strong sympathy with the peasantry of
the realm,' he wrote, ' had been one of the characteristic sensibilities of Lord Henry at Eton.   Yet a
schoolboy, he had busied himself with their pastimes
and the details of their cottage economy.   As he
advanced in life the horizon of his views expanded
with his intelligence and his experience ; . . . and
on the very threshold of his career he devoted his time
and thought, labour and life, to one vast and noble
purpose, the elevation of the condition of the great
body of the people.'   Of keener intellect and of
far less stable character than Lord John, George
Smythe raised the highest hopes among his contemporaries.   A man of ideas and of a quick originality, he might have won distinction in many fields.
He has left behind him fragments of literature which
may still be read with pleasure.   It will give some
measure of his charm and humour if we say that
throughout his wayward life he retained unabated
the affection of Lord John Manners, and that Disraeli
owned he ' was the only man who had never bored
him.'   His friendship with his two closest colleagues
lasted till the day of his death, and Disraeli painted his
portrait more than once with candour and admiration.
He sat for Coningsby, and he is the Waldershare of
Endymion—' profligate but sentimental, unprincipled
but romantic ; the child of whim, and the slave of an
imagination so freakish and deceptive that it was

always impossible to foretell his course. He was alike capable of sacrificing all his feelings to worldly considerations, or of forfeiting the world for a visionary caprice.'

Thus Disraeli, and perhaps it is by paradoxes that Smythe may best be described.   His career itself was a paradox in which genius and failure are closely interwoven.   Perhaps he loved life too well ; perhaps he cared too little for life's wise management to win what is called success.   Certain it is that in a worldly sense he failed brilliantly and completely. His failure does but set a keen edge upon the memory of his wit.   There is often an element of dulness in success, if another paradox be permitted, and George Smythe was never dull.   He passed through life like a brilliant butterfly, and if he left it with smirched wings, he lived always in the sunshine of a gay popularity.

Such were the men who were the first to serve under Disraeli's leadership.   Their banner belonged to them all ; the leadership was Disraeli's own. Others there were who stood or sat by their side— Cochrane and Baillie,—and at Deepdene they indulged their fancy as they would.   The new party won an instant recognition.   It was indeed the wonder of a season.   It gave its name to a foolish newspaper ; its praise or blame was on every tongue ; and its importance for Disraeli was that it helped to accentuate his obvious divergence from official Toryism.   For Young England Peel's autocratic temper could

profess no sympathy.   The generous aspirations of
Manners and Smythe were unintelligible to his
practical common-sense, and it is clear that he already
regarded Disraeli as his bitterest enemy.   'With
respect to Young England,' he wrote to Croker, 'the
puppets are moved by Disraeli, who is the ablest man
among them : I consider him unprincipled and
disappointed, and in despair he has tried the effect
of bullying.   I think with you they will return to the
crib after prancing, capering, and snorting ; but a
crack or two of the whip well applied may hasten and
ensure their return.   Disraeli alone is mischievous,
and with him I have no desire to keep terms.   It were
better for the party if he were driven into the ranks of
our open enemies.'   This letter was written in 1843,
and it proves that Peel was still groping in the dark.
In three years he was destined himself to smash the
party, and it was Disraeli, and no legitimate heir of his,
who was called upon to reshape it.

The definite achievement of Young England was
not great.   It did not change the course of English
politics ; it did not sensibly improve the condition of
the working-classes.   It held meetings at Manchester
and Bingley, which gave its members an opportunity
of much eloquence.   It did what it could to encourage
Athenæums, as the homes of popular culture were
called, and to further an excellent scheme of allotments.
This is not much, it may be said ; but Young England
did far more than may be precisely measured.   It gave
a humaner tone to politics ; it reminded the country

K

that the condition of the people was not merely 'a knife and fork question,' that ' you must cultivate the heart as well as seek to content the belly ' ; it insisted that the things of the mind were worth fighting for, and that the distinctions of class, eagerly cultivated by the Whigs, were no sound basis for society. The teaching of Disraeli and his noble-hearted friends has, alas ! been long ago forgotten. To-day an appeal to anything but a knife and fork falls upon deaf ears, and there is none to inaugurate another party of Young England. As there were then generous souls to speak, there were generous souls also to listen. Though the party was broken, a part at least of its work was done. Upon Disraeli and his career, as we have said, it had a conspicuous influence. It gave him a wise, foreseeing policy, and it placed him in direct opposition to Peel. And then it inspired *Coningsby*.

There is no episode in Disraeli's life that has been more fiercely discussed than his relations with Peel, and it is only just to treat these relations at considerable length. At the outset Disraeli, like the rest of his generation, was disposed to welcome Peel as the hope and stay of the Tory party. He was delighted at Peel's approval, and smiled gaily in the light of his countenance. Great was his satisfaction when Wyndham Lewis declared that ' Peel had taken him by the hand in a most marked manner.' The applause of his leader was grateful in his ears and freely given. His maiden speech was encouraged by none more

loyally than by Peel. ' Sir Robert Peel,' we are told,
' who very rarely cheers any honourable gentleman,
not even the most able and accomplished speaker of
his own party, greeted Mr. Disraeli's speech with a
prodigality of applause which must have been very
trying to the worthy baronet's lungs. . . . He
repeatedly turned round his head, and looking the
youthful orator in the face, cheered him in the most
stentorian tones.' Two years later Disraeli still
took pleasure in the friendship of Peel. ' I dined at
Sir Robert's on Saturday,' he wrote to his sister, ' and
came late, having mistaken the hour. I found some
twenty-five gentlemen grubbing in solemn silence. I
threw a shot over the table and set them going, and in
time they became even noisy. Peel, I think, was
quite pleased that I broke the awful stillness, as he
talked to me a good deal, though we were far removed.'
Disraeli, of course, preserved his independence : he
spoke and voted on occasion against his party, but
with no more violence than was permitted to a young
Member of Parliament.

All went well indeed until 1841, when Peel once
more became Prime Minister, and Disraeli applied,
as well he might, for the recognition which he thought
due to him. The letter which he wrote to Peel was
insistent and a trifle sentimental. ' I confess to be
unrecognised at this moment by you appears to me to
be overwhelming, and I appeal to your own heart—
to that justice and magnanimity which I feel are your
characteristics—to save me from an intolerable humilia-

tion.' The answer was what we should expect—
cold and conclusive. ' I trust,' replied Peel, ' that,
when candidates for Parliamentary office calmly reflect
on my position and the appointments I have made,
they will understand how perfectly insufficient are
the means at my disposal to meet the wishes that are
conveyed to me by men whose co-operation I should be
proud to have, and whose qualifications and preten-
sions for office I do not contest.' Both wrote the
letters that we should expect of them. The worst of
it was that each was incapable of understanding the
other. Peel, never a keen judge of men, put too low
a value upon Disraeli's eminent ability. Disraeli,
conscious of his power, was impatient of delay

In Peel's favour it may be said that Disraeli had
been less than four years in Parliament, and that
though he had proved himself a clear and courageous
speaker, though he was already a master of political
history and political tactics, he had not yet won the
universal ear of the House. Applauded vigorously by
a clique, he was looked upon askance by many on either
side. Even three years later, he was not generally
accepted. He was still paying dearly for the means
by which he had advanced. By a stroke of ill-luck,
he seemed always an easy mark for slander. Many
a foolish libel, now disproved and still believed, was
circulated to his discredit. ' Nor, in spite of all his
gifts,' Mr. Monypenny writes, ' had he yet acquired
the authentic House of Commons manner. He had
courage and originality, unbounded cleverness, and that

most effective weapon—the power of sarcasm. But all these are gifts which require supreme tact for their judicious display in Parliament, and in Parliamentary tact he was at first a little wanting. . . . There was an element of pretentiousness and presumption in his speeches which the House of Commons resented. The oracular manner, which became a positive asset when he reached a high position, tended to delay his ascent. He was too didactic in tone, and his cleverness, though great, was too ostentatious.' That is true enough, and had he been given office, the responsibility would doubtless have sobered his manner. He did not get office, and though it is not for us to regret an exclusion which gave us *Coningsby* and *Sybil*, it was clear that for him the political battle was to fight again.

Though Disraeli was disappointed of office, it is plain that his divergence from the Government was in no way inspired by injured vanity. It was Peel who changed throughout, not he. He was elected by his constituents to protect the landed interest, and faithfully he performed his trust. As early as 1843 he suspected any motion which meant ' that they should fight against hostile tariffs with free imports,'— a policy bound to end in disaster. Valiantly did he come to the rescue of Mr. Gladstone, ' my right hon. friend, the Vice-President of the Board of Trade,' by pleading for the happy medium, followed by practical men, the principle of reciprocity. Before his constituents he used the same language as he used in the House. ' Shall I tell you,' said he at Shrewsbury, speaking of the great Rebellion, 'how it was that the nation returned to itself, and Old England after the deluge was seen rising above the waters ?   This was the reason—because during all that fearful revolution you never changed the tenure of your landed property. That, I think, gentlemen, proves my case ; and if we have baffled a wit like Oliver Cromwell, let us not be staggered even before Mr. Cobden.'   Though, in the event, an alliance between Peel and Cobden proved too strong for the landed interest, they who would suggest a malice in Disraeli's conflict with Peel over-look the plain facts of the case.   A Member of Parliament is not bound to change with his leaders, even though office be refused him.

Then followed the interval of Young England, and clearly Peel and his friends were stung to fury. Graham wished to drive Disraeli into open hostility —a hostility which, when it came, they endured with an ill grace.   A letter of Peel's obviously exhibits the politician's point of view.   'I am very glad,' wrote Peel in December 1843, 'that Mr. Disraeli has asked for an office for his brother.   It is a good thing when such a man puts his shabbiness on record.   He asked me for office for himself, and I was not surprised that being refused he became independent and a patriot. But to ask favours after his conduct of last session is too bad.   However, it is a bridle in his mouth.'   Alas, for Peel's peace of mind !   It was not a bridle.   It could not be a bridle, because Disraeli was resolved to put his principles into practice.   The support of

Young England, the writing of *Sybil* and *Coningsby*, had helped him to evolve the Tory idea. Of this idea henceforth he was the constant champion. He hoped, as we have said, to see England once more possess a free monarchy and a privileged and prosperous people. He would have nothing to do with Arch-Mediocrities and Venetian Doges. He asked for faith in a political doctrine, and he heard on all sides nothing but the Opportunism of Peel. 'The Tamworth Manifesto of 1835,' he wrote, 'was an attempt to construct a party without principles; its basis, therefore, was necessarily Latitudinarianism, and its inevitable consequence has been Political Infidelity.' He fought the battle of the people and the landed gentry against the greedy encroachment of the middle-class. He defeated Peel, and fell himself before the forces combined against him. He fell only for a moment, and at least a spark of his imaginative faith still shines in the dusty air of politics.

The battle between Disraeli and Peel, which began in 1845, is unique in our annals. At first sight it seemed as though the combatants were ill-matched. Disraeli had never held office. The prestige of an ancient and successful Minister clung about Peel. He played upon the House of Commons 'as upon an old fiddle.' If he could not rise to the highest flights of oratory, he was a perfect master of the clear statement. In brief, 'what he really was,' as Disraeli said, 'and what posterity will acknowledge him to have been, is the greatest Member of Parliament that ever lived.' His worst failing, and it was bad indeed, was an impulsive variability. He 'had a peculiarity,' wrote his adversary, 'which is perhaps natural with men of very great talents who have not the creative faculty : he had a dangerous sympathy with the creations of others.' And having suddenly accepted the opinion or the plan of another, he attempted to force it forthwith upon all his supporters. Not to change at the same instant at which he changed, was in his eyes the blackest treachery. The example of Peel has been generally followed since his time.

When Mr. Gladstone's thumb pricked for the cause of Home Rule, every Radical thumb in Great Britain was expected to prick. And the witless docility of Members of Parliament has more often brought the House of Commons into disrepute than the habit of rebellion. In 1845 independence was not yet an extinct virtue, and Disraeli opposed to Peel all the qualities which that Minister lacked. In the first place, he came forward as the champion of a principle. He had mastered the gospel which he meant to preach, and he wasted no words in vague exposition. He was as high in courage as he was firm in resolution. He was, moreover, an oratorical light-horseman whom few could resist. He understood perfectly the conduct of those dangerous weapons—irony and sarcasm. As a master of phrases which cut and slashed and left an unforgettable wound, he had no rival in his own day. And when he faced Peel in single combat, there should have been hardly any doubt as to the issue.

In the first encounter Peel made a slip, for which he paid dearly.   He was indiscreet enough in making a retort upon Disraeli to quote some lines by Canning, of whom his treatment was still remembered in the House.   Disraeli was not one to lose his chance. 'The right hon. gentleman,' he said, 'may be sure that such a quotation from such an authority will always tell.   Some lines, for example, upon friendship, written by Mr. Canning, and quoted by the right hon. gentleman !   The theme, the poet, the speaker— what a felicitous combination ! '   The effect of this speech of Disraeli's was immediate.   His first Philippic, as Mr. Monypenny calls it, gave him a far higher position in the House than that to which he had attained.   ' It would have made you cry with delight,' wrote George Smythe to Mrs. Disraeli, ' to have heard the thunders of cheering.'   It seemed as though the battle was already won.   Disraeli was pitiless and exultant.   Night after night he assailed his foe with hard logic and brilliant satire.   If only Peel had hit back, the contest would seem yet more splendid than it does.   On the one hand, Disraeli gave no quarter ; on the other, Peel hardly dared to resist. Mr. Gladstone declared fifty years afterwards that Peel tried to answer only once, and then ' failed utterly.'

That the victory was well deserved there can be no doubt.   In dialectic, as in oratory, Disraeli proved himself easily Peel's superior.   There is nothing that so easily loses its savour as Parliamentary speeches. Made for the moment, they rarely outlive the moment for which they are made.   Nobody will ever again read a single speech of Peel's or Gladstone's. Disraeli's Philippics are as fresh as on the day of their delivery.   They have taken their place, with certain orations by Demosthenes and Cicero, among the masterpieces of invective.   So familiar are they to the most of us, that as we read them we seem to be turning over the pages of a book of elegant extracts. They contain phrases which are a permanent enrichment of our speech, which have passed into the heritage of our blood and state.   ' The right hon. gentleman caught the Whigs bathing and walked away with their clothes.   He has left them in the full enjoyment of their liberal position, and he is himself a strict conservative of their garments.'   That gem sparkled in the first of the attacking speeches, and its radiance is still undimmed.   The truth is that Disraeli was what is very rare among politicians, a man of letters.   He was born in a library, and though he had not the industry always to chasten his unwritten prose, a sense of literature did not desert him even on the hustings. In the speeches which he delivered against Peel, you cannot but be amazed at the conciseness of his phrase and the justice of his imagery.   These are not the qualities, maybe, which ensured the instant triumph of his speeches.   They are the qualities which have endowed those speeches with a lasting life and interest.

Meanwhile Peel was approaching nearer and nearer to that policy of Free Trade which his Cabinet was pledged to oppose, and Disraeli's invective never

lacked an opportunity.   ' I remember the right hon.
gentleman making his protection speeches,' said
Disraeli in a famous attack.   ' They were the best
speeches I ever heard.   It was a great thing to hear
the right hon. gentleman say :   " I would rather be
the leader of the gentlemen of England than possess
the confidence of Sovereigns."   That was a grand
thing.   We don't hear much of " the gentlemen of
England " now.'   And so he came to the peroration,
which still seems to echo in our ears : ' For myself, I
care not what may be the result.   Dissolve, if you
please, the Parliament you have betrayed, and appeal
to the people, who, I believe, mistrust you.   For
me there remains this at least—the opportunity of
expressing thus publicly my belief that a Conservative
Government is an organised hypocrisy.'   Nor are we
likely to forget the expression of his contempt for the
Minister who founds great measures upon small pre-
cedents :   ' He always traced the steam-engine back
to the tea-kettle.'   And then his description of the
Parliamentary middleman, is it not superb ?—' It is
well known what a middleman is : he is a man who
bamboozles one party and plunders the other, till,
having obtained a position to which he is not entitled,
he cries out, " Let us have no party questions, but
fixity of tenure." '

When in 1845 Peel resigned, only to receive again
the poisoned chalice, which Lord John Russell handed
back to him, Disraeli had still better ground for his
attack, and found in Lord George Bentinck the

staunchest of allies.   Nothing but political trickery,
the desire of hanging on to office at all hazards, could
justify the step which Peel now took.   Even he must
have found it hard to convince himself that the failure
of the potato crop in Ireland was a fair reason for
throwing open the ports of England to foreign corn
three years hence.   It was Cobden whom Peel had
caught bathing this time, and whose clothes he had
stolen.   Disraeli rose with the occasion, and the best
of all his speeches were made in the fight of 1845-6.
He poured the wealth of his scorn and ridicule upon
' the political pedlars that bought their party in the
cheapest market and sold us in the dearest.'   He
avowed himself no enemy of Free Trade, but he
explained again and again the futility of attempting
to fight hostile tariffs with Free Imports.   And then
there was the magnificent passage about Popkins's
plan.   ' And is England to be governed,' he asked,
' and is England to be convulsed by Popkins's plan ?
Will he go to the country with it ?   Will he go with
it to that ancient and famous England that was once
governed by statesmen—by Burleighs and by Walsing-
hams ; by Bolingbrokes and by Walpoles ; by a
Chatham and a Canning,—will he go to it with this
fantastic scheming of some presumptuous pedant ? '
Seldom has the artifice of contrast been more happily
employed, and it is not strange that the sally was
received with ' peals of laughter from all parts of the
House.'

Nor can we pass over in silence the incident which,

more than any other in his career, throws a shadow
upon the character of Disraeli.   Peel, stung beyond
endurance, made the one effective reply of the whole
campaign.   He asked how it was, if he were guilty
of petty larcenies, that Disraeli was prepared to give
him his support in 1841.   ' It is still more surprising,'
he added, ' that he should have been ready, as I think
he was, to unite his fortunes with mine in office, thus
implying the strongest proof which any public man can
give of confidence in the honour and integrity of a
Minister of the Crown.'   Peel's retort was perfectly
fair, and might have been fairly met.   It would have
been easy for Disraeli to point out that the Peel of
1846 was not the Peel of 1841, whom he had been
prepared to support and to serve—that in the five
elapsing years Peel had sacrificed all his cherished
principles and had turned his back upon the declared
policy of the Tory party.   Unfortunately Disraeli
did not do this.   Instead, he was guilty of what will
always seem the most discreditable utterance of his
life.   He denied that he had ever asked of Peel the
smallest favour.   ' I never shall,' said he,—' it is
totally foreign to my nature—make an application for
any place.'   Was it forgetfulness or falsehood ?
Even if we take it at its worst—as perhaps we are
bound to do—it is a sin which most politicians would
commit with a light heart.   There is always an off-
chance that an incriminating letter may be lost, and
in the rough-and-tumble of politics, scruples, I fear,
are never too finely edged.   ' Let the politician,' says

Mr. Monypenny, 'who is without sin in the matter of veracity cast the first stone.'

Thus the battle had been fought with only one wrong blow on the part of Disraeli, and the discomfiture of Peel was complete. 'They had trooped : all the men of metal and large-acred squires,' into the lobby hostile to their leader. Peel was left, like Napoleon after Moscow, 'without his army.' Artistically, oratorically, morally, the victory remained with Disraeli. I say 'morally,' because I agree with Mr. Monypenny that 'there is not only a moral but an intellectual integrity, and in the intellectual virtue Peel was as much the inferior of Disraeli as in the moral he was his superior.' It is easy to wish that Disraeli had not made a false declaration. It is impossible to acquit Peel of the charge that he betrayed the lifelong convictions of himself and his colleagues. However, with Peel's retirement the organised hypocrisy was swept away, and Disraeli never again spoke a harsh word about him.

Indeed, the more that is discovered of Disraeli and his career, the more readily are we convinced of his honour and integrity. Truly of him it may be said that to know all is to know how little there is to pardon. He has been blamed, for instance, by those whose interest it was to cover him with insult, that he married his wife mainly for her money. There is no more deeply interesting chapter in Mr. Monypenny's book than that in which he allows Disraeli to tell the story of his courtship and marriage. Both husband and

wife come out bravely from the ordeal of publicity ;
and if an honourable man has been relieved of reproach,
the portrait of an admirably loyal and devoted woman is
well and truly drawn. Thus we arrive at the turning-
point of Disraeli's career. Fierce in opposition,
supreme in invective, the coldest critic of another's
conduct that Parliament has known since the Cornet
of Horse, he is destined presently to exchange the free
courage of a light-horseman for the responsibilities of
leadership. Nor did he fall when the hour of danger
came.

III.—INTERLUDE

After the storm of 1846 there was a calm in the
career of Benjamin Disraeli. The orator's attack
upon Peel had had its due effect, and the powerful
Minister had been forced to resign in the hour of
victory on the battle-field. But much else besides Sir
Robert Peel's supremacy had perished. The party
of Protection had demolished its adversary, it is true,
but had fallen itself in the general ruin, like Samson
in the temple. If Peel, for his part, had destroyed
the great Tory party, he had left no policy for either
party to defend or attack. The Corn Laws were
repealed, and it seemed as though the fight must be
fought over again on the same ground. On the
one hand, the Manchester School, having effectually
' lowered the tone ' of English life, had neither the
power nor the desire to construct, and on the other,
the champions of Protection seemed to have no better

prospect than that of attempting to put together
the broken pieces of a shattered edifice. Disraeli,
at the outset, cherished the vain hope of reaction.
Encouraged by the adamantine resolution of Lord
George Bentinck, he thought that, since Peel had
been overthrown, the work that he had achieved
might be undone.

Soon doubt and uncertainty crept into his mind.
'The past is a dream,' he wrote, 'and the future
a mystery. I cannot read it.' Time brought a swift
piercing of the mystery. Disraeli awoke from the
dream of the past, and discovered that the future
belonged not to the visionary but to the practical
politician. He was no longer the freelance who had
led Young England and broken the power of Sir
Robert Peel. With the increasing gravity of his
purpose he assumed a graver demeanour. 'According to a descriptive writer,' says Mr. Buckle,
'Disraeli changed more than his seat. He modified
the extravagance of his clothing. The "motley-
coloured garments," which he still wore at the close
of the session of 1846, were exchanged for a suit of
black, "unapproachably perfect" in every stitch, "and
he appears to have doffed the vanity of the coxcomb
with the plumage of the peacock." He was also
thought to have acquired a weightier manner of
speaking, suited to his more responsible position.'

The changes thus hinted corresponded accurately
to a change of mind. Disraeli knew better than most
of his contemporaries that politics is a game which must

be played in accord with certain rules. There are
always supporters to be conciliated, animosities to be
soothed, policies to be adapted to the exigencies of the
moment. To have fought the battle of Protection
over again would have been to ensure disaster, and
Disraeli very soon saw that no good end would be
served by undoing what Peel had done. After all,
the Corn Laws had been repealed by majorities in the
two Houses. The Constitution had not been outraged by the repeal, as it has been outraged since by
those who passed the iniquitous Parliament Act, and
Disraeli believed it to be the duty of a good citizen
to acquiesce in the accomplished fact. In 1847 he
addressed the electors of Buckingham and made his
position quite clear. 'I am not one of those,' he
wrote, 'who would counsel or who would abet any
attempt factiously and forcibly to repeal the measures
of 1846. The legislative sanction which they have
obtained requires that they should receive an ample
experiment ; and I am persuaded that this test alone
can satisfy the nation either of their expediency or their
want of fitness.' It is not that he had renounced
Protection in his heart. It is probable that he remained a Protectionist unto the end of his life, and
fearing, as he did, a policy of Free Imports, he
preserved a faith in reciprocity. Meanwhile, he
recognised that in practice Protection was 'not only
dead but damned,' and he meant, above all things, to
be a practical politician.

To this view he adhered with the utmost firmness,

L

and in spite of the obstinacy of certain colleagues, what he said in 1847 he repeated in a slightly different form in 1852. Admitting still the soundness of Protection, ' if the country has chosen to abrogate that system,' said he, ' and if the majority of the people of this country are of opinion that it would be unwise to recur to it, I say we must seek by other means, and in another direction, to place the cultivators of the soil in a fair and just position.' The reasonableness of these words cannot be contested, and Disraeli, writing in 1860, looked back upon his achievement with satisfaction. Here is the account which he gave of his early leadership, and the fairness of which none will contest : ' I found the Tory Party in the House of Commons,' thus he wrote, ' when I acceded to its chief management, in a state of great depression and disorganisation. Lord George Bentinck had only mustered one hundred and twenty on his motion on the Irish Railways, which was to try our strength in the new Parliament. By a series of motions to relieve the Agricultural Interest by revising and partially removing the local taxation of the country, I withdrew the Tory Party gradually from the hopeless question of Protection, rallied all those members who were connected . . . with the land, and finally brought the state of parties in the House of Commons to a tie.'

It was a great triumph, which it needed all Disraeli's tact and courage to achieve. The withdrawal of Protection alone was enough to daunt a less courageous man. Disraeli could not say a word upon the vexed

question without alienating some support. Though
Protection were dead in the country, it still retained
many warm champions in the Commons. Stanley
himself, Disraeli's own chief, was a thick-and-thin
believer in the ancient and righteous cult. What,
then, was Disraeli to do ? Was he to desert his
leader or to lose the sympathy of the rank and file ?
Was he to keep on good terms with Mr. Young and
the Protection Society, or to loosen his hold upon the
House ? You have not to look far for proofs of the
statesman's delicate position. That he should have
won his own way in the end was a foregone conclusion.
It took him some ten years of thankless work to
complete the education of his party.

And by the irony of politics, at the very moment that
Disraeli was fighting their battle, the Peelites and
Cobdenites fell upon him with renewed bitterness.
Having won in the fight of Free Trade, these politicians knew no other cause which they might espouse,
and so they guarded their victory with a jealous fury,
as though it were about to be snatched from them.
If they had had their way, whatever was left of English
history should have been one long, uninterrupted
triumph. They would have been content to go from
platform to platform celebrating Peel's conquest of
Protection. And when Disraeli declared that he had
no wish to abrogate the Acts of 1846, they either
refused to believe him or were enraged that the Aunt
Sally, at which they hoped to hurl their brickbats, was
ravished from them. Instead of rallying to Disraeli,

because he had come over to their side, they declared that whatever he said was untrue, whatever he did was cunning.   Mr. Gladstone and the Peelites, no doubt, were moved by the anger of revenge against the man who in his famous Philippics had triumphantly demolished their leader.   The Cobdenites, with whom Disraeli had a certain curious sympathy, assailed him as sentimentalists always assail that which they do not understand.   For them Free Trade was not a policy ; it was a religion.   They held it sacred as the Ark of the Covenant, and when Disraeli told them that it was an 'accident,' for a while beyond the reach of criticism, they repelled such overtures as he permitted himself to make with anger and contempt.

The attacks upon Disraeli's Budget of 1852, for instance, were inspired rather by malevolence than by mere disapproval.   It was a Free Trade Budget, which leaned naturally upon direct taxation, and in principle differed little enough from the Budget which covered Mr. Gladstone with glory a year later.   But it was Disraeli's Budget, and it was therefore attacked most acrimoniously by Wood, Graham, and Gladstone, who might have supported it had it borne another's name.   Disraeli, always fearless in defence, had no difficulty in annihilating the arguments of his opponents.   They had not spared him in attack, and he had no scruple in lashing them as he thought they deserved.   It was for Wood that he reserved the keenest edge of his satire.   'But then the right honourable gentleman tells me,' said he, 'in not very polished, and scarcely in Parliamentary language, that I do not know my business. He may have learned his business. The House of Commons is the best judge of that ; I care not to be his critic. Yet, if he has learned his business, he has still to learn some other things—he has to learn that petulance is not sarcasm, and that insolence is not invective.' And again : ' I have been told to withdraw my Budget. I was told that Mr. Pitt withdrew his Budget, and I know that more recently other persons have done so too. Sir, I do not aspire to the fame of Mr. Pitt, but '—speaking in a louder tone, and with a finger pointed at Wood —' I will not submit to the degradation of others.'

Though Disraeli was left with the honours of debate, the Coalition proved too strong for him, and his Budget was flung into the limbo of forgotten things. Thither it was flung, not for any demerits of its own, but because Disraeli himself had contrived to earn the dislike of several ill-connected cliques. Malice makes stranger bed-fellows than adversity, and Derby was quite right when he declared that it was a personal pique which destroyed the financial measure of 1852. And as we look back upon the speeches and arguments of seventy years ago, we cannot but wonder at the slow progress made by Disraeli in the business of politics. The ten years of this interlude are the active years of a statesman's life. And at the end of them, when he was past fifty, Disraeli is only on the threshold of success. Few men have ever taken a quicker brain, a firmer courage into the political arena ; assuredly no man ever was asked to wait so long for a legitimate reward.

When Peel resigned in 1846, Disraeli already dominated the House of Commons with his eloquence. In 1855 he had but begun to dominate his party. The obstacles which lay in his path were many and various. He did not belong to a great house ; he had no lofty connections. He had fought for his own hand and with his own weapons, which were not always agreeable to his opponents. When George Bentinck died, he should have been accepted without question or delay as the leader of the Tory party, then against his will acquiring for the first time the familiar name of Conservative. Stanley, who led the forces in the House of Lords, still preserved a profound distrust of his illustrious colleague. He could not afford to lose his support ; he dared not place the destinies of the party unreservedly in his hands. So he hedged him about with restrictions, made him not the supreme head in the Commons, but one of a triumvirate, and refused to recognise the plain fact that the leader is always the man who leads, not the unfortunate chosen in the vague hope that he may lead some day.

Moreover, Disraeli was not merely a politician without connections : he was also a militant Jew. There is no doubt that his championship of his own people did not a little to break in pieces the party of Protection. By a stroke of purposed ill-luck Lord John Russell brought in his motion to admit Jews to Parliament at a time when the stalwart few led by

George Bentinck and Disraeli were not wholly at one. Those who were keenest for Protection wavered in their views of Church discipline, and the supporters of the Tractarian movement were apt to set their theological opinions higher in the scale than their hatred of Free Trade. The speech which Disraeli delivered on behalf of his own people was a bomb-shell. It disconcerted all his friends of the High Church, and added not a jot of strength to the cause of Protection. Against the eloquence and ingenuity of Disraeli's plea there may have been, from his point of view, no word to be said. He was a Jew, proud of Jewry, pleading for the Jews. ' It will be seen,' said he, ' that all the tendencies of the Jewish race are conservative. Their bias is to religion, property, and natural aristocracy ; and it should be the interest of statesmen that this bias of a great race should be encouraged, and their energies and creative powers enlisted in the cause of existing society.' The challenge, implied in these words, was thrown down by Disraeli the Jew, not by Disraeli the statesman. When Disraeli touched upon the religious argument, his statement was wholly provocative. To profess the whole Jewish faith is, said he, ' to believe in Calvary as well as in Sinai.'

His celebrated peroration was not devised to strengthen the waverer. ' Has not He made their history,' he asked, ' the most famous in the world ? Has not He hung up their laws in every temple ? Has not He vindicated all their wrongs ?   Has not

He avenged the victory of Titus and conquered the
Cæsars ? What successes did they anticipate from
their Messiah ? The wildest dreams of their rabbis
have been far exceeded. Has not Jesus conquered
Europe and changed its name into Christendom ?
All countries which refuse the Cross wither, while the
whole of the new world is devoted to the Semitic
principle, and its most glorious offspring, the Jewish
faith. . . . Christians may continue to persecute Jews,
and Jews may persist in disbelieving Christians, but
who can deny that Jesus of Nazareth, the Incarnate
Son of the Most High God, is the eternal glory of the
Jewish race ? ' It is excellent rhetoric, and yet of no
effect. It is acceptable neither to Christians nor to
Jews. For it leaves out of sight the two truths, that
the Jews crucified Jesus, and have declined for nearly
two thousand years to put their faith in Him. They
have withered, as all peoples have withered, which,
in Disraeli's own words, refuse the Cross.

That Disraeli should have defended the race from
which he sprang is natural. It is not a little
strange that he should have missed the point of his
own argument. He preaches in *Tancred* and elsewhere the romantic doctrine that ' all is race.' All *is*
race—that is true. But the race of which Disraeli
spoke and wrote is the Jewish race, and the race which
he aspired to govern was the English race. It would
be easy to turn the reasoning against him, and to resent
the intrusion in our counsels of one who was not of
our own blood. That is what the politicians of seventy

years ago did, and by their folly long excluded from the
leadership the farthest-sighted statesman of his time.
That is what the most of us would do to-day, and with
excellent reason, because a Disraeli nowhere confronts
us.   An excuse may be found for the Tory of that
age.   He did not perceive that Disraeli was lifted
far above the superstition of blood.   He belonged not
to England nor to Palestine.   He was akin to the
great of all times and places.   It was only in the
foibles and vanities of life that he betrayed the signs
of his origin.   He had not the qualities which are
commonly associated with the Jewish race.   In a
country of brave men he was conspicuous for his
courage.   He was never tired of urging upon Stanley
the bold course.   He was content always to take risks,
and to fight for his own hand, his own party.   Nor did
he display the smallest interest in money, except for
the influence it might purchase him.   The acquisition of Hughenden proved a recklessness which we
might reasonably expect in an Englishman bred to
take the chances of the turf.   Nevertheless he had
a natural love of perplexity : he delighted to confuse
the slow understanding of some of his colleagues ; and
if the squires of England failed at first to trust and
appreciate him, let it be remembered that he threw
the dust of the Asian Mystery in their puzzled eyes.

Whatever else he was, he was a statesman.   He
divined the art of governance.   His mind was quick
with prophecies and intuitions.   It has been said,
on the strength of one petulant phrase, that he

had little interest in the Colonies.   A study of his career will instantly remove this absurd misunderstanding.   Not only was his devotion to our Colonial Empire sincerely grounded, but his views as to the necessity of knitting closer the bonds which bound them to us prove him a prophet.   Here is a profession of faith made in 1850 : ' If we wish,' said he, ' to maintain our political power or our commercial wealth, we can only secure these great results by the consolidation of our Colonial Empire.   I will not advert to the political means by which such a consolidation might be maintained.   I will not enter into the difficult but important consideration whether the Colonies ought or ought not to be represented in this House— although these are questions which we ought not to discard from our minds—but looking only to the commercial and fiscal part of the subject, I cannot understand by what means in the present day, following the current of our recent legislation, the consolidation can take place unless we can reduce into a fact a phrase which political economists are so fond of using— namely, that our Colonies should be placed on the same footing as the Counties of England.'

Thus he was already—in 1850—a convert of the doctrine of Colonial Preference ; and if he had had his way, or had found in Stanley a more energetic colleague, he would have devised some method by which the Colonies should be represented in a truly Imperial Parliament. To Lord Derby he put the question with great force and clearness in 1851.

' Is it impossible to make a great push,' he asked,
' founded much on the alarming state of Europe and
the consequently unstable character of our foreign
trade, to reconstruct our Colonial system, or rather
Empire, by freeing the Colonies from all duties,
or some other mode, and conceding to them as
represented in the Imperial Parliament the vacancy
occasioned by the disfranchised boroughs, so bringing
a third element formally into the House, and healing
that too obvious division and rivalry between town
and country ? '   If it is a crude sketch, it contains
all the ideas which in the last sixty years have been
held by the passionate champions of our Colonial
Empire.   Unhappily, Derby was not of those who
make ' great pushes,' and Disraeli's sketch never
grew into the finished drawing of his imagination.

While we may survey Disraeli on many sides and
in many lights, we can never doubt Disraeli's grasp
of foreign affairs and of foreign policy.   It was not
for a whim that Louis Philippe called him a friend,
or that Metternich hailed him as a colleague in the
great task of ' conservation.'   Disraeli had travelled
widely and felt not the narrowness of insularity.
Though not an accomplished linguist, he knew France
as he knew England, and it was upon a knowledge
of France that his foreign policy was based.   He
believed first and foremost in a cordial understanding
with France, and when he first took office as Chancellor of the Exchequer, he hoped to frame a commercial treaty with that country.   At the same time

he was sure that it was the best chance of prosperity that every country should develop in proper accord with its own character and traditions.   He condemned bitterly the ideal of uniformity which Lord Palmerston and the Radicals had set up in the face of Europe. 'You looked upon the English Constitution as a model farm,' he said.   'You forced this Constitution in every country.   You laid it down as a great principle that you were not to consider the interests of England, or the interests of the country you were in connection with, but you were to consider the great system of Liberalism, which had nothing to do with the interests of England, and was generally antagonistic to the interests of the country with which you were in connection.'   In these wise words he demolished a superstition of foreign policy, which still exists furtively in our midst, and flourishes exceedingly in the United States of America.

As the career of Disraeli is unfolded, our impression deepens and widens of his skill in attack.   He was an awkward adversary, as Peel and Gladstone knew, and there is no better example of his method than his cruel and efficient mangling of the Coalition which committed us to the Crimean War.   He would not move a want of confidence in them, said he, because they had no confidence in themselves.   That Palmerston and Aberdeen and Lord John Russell should attempt to row in the same boat was at once their shame and their ineptitude.   Nor was their position made any surer or any saner by the fact that they held together, a disconnected gang, merely because they hated Disraeli. This was the one point of their union, and Disraeli, knowing it, spared them not.

That he did not take too light a view of their shortcomings is evident from the baneful result of their policy. They drifted into war because they could agree upon nothing else, and they saved their places on the Treasury Bench, as others since have done, merely because the country showed a firm front in the face of national peril. And whether he attacked or defended, Disraeli, as I have said, was always a man of letters. The literary touch is absent neither from his speeches nor his letters. Nor is it difficult to discover how it is that in the general oblivion of politicians he survives almost alone. It is style, it is wit that has kept alive his lightest utterances. You have but to compare his letters, for instance, with Derby's to measure his superiority. And it remains a paradox of politics that a man of genius, so brilliantly endowed as was Disraeli, should find himself at the age of fifty-one still insecure and with no longer a period of office behind him than a few brief months. His day, maliciously deferred, came at last, and they who had been as stumbling-blocks in his path were only too willing to share in the glory, when he had reached the goal.

IV.—LEADERSHIP

If Disraeli's career in the 'fifties and 'sixties seems, for the moment, of less interest than what went before or came after, it is because the Great War has cast an ominous shadow upon politics. A time of crisis discovers the futility of politicians as surely as a once famous serum revealed in its victims the imminence of phthisis. In other words, it diagnoses and does not cure. To-day we know only too well that the Ministers, in whose hands reposed the destiny of our Empire, refused to warn or to prepare. They resembled a watchman who, seeing a house on fire, obstinately kept his peace, lest perchance he might arouse the sleeper within. And not unnaturally the disaster, which caught us unawares, colours in our mind the politics of the past. After all, we see with regret that the game is played not for the nation but for the players, who are only too ready to sacrifice the public interest to their passionate desire for place. As we look back on these years of transition which came between the Crimean War and Disraeli's Reform Bill, we cannot but be conscious of a kind of futility. After peace was made with Russia, after the Indian Mutiny was quelled, there is little to record, save the attempts which either side made to reform the franchise, and the attacks, happily repelled, which the Radicals aimed at the Church of England. For the rest the two parties in the State were so near in agreement, there was so little difference between the 'ins' and 'outs,' that the battle in the House of Commons was a battle rather of rhetoric than of principle. When Palmerston and Disraeli were opposed to one another, both Tories of the old school, both fervent believers

in our English tradition, it was eloquence matched
with eloquence, not opinion assailing opinion.   In
this mimic contest there was room neither for the display of invective nor for the exposition of political
philosophy.   The two men agreed in strategy.   They
differed in tactics.

It is characteristic of Disraeli that in three barren
years he never lost heart and he never lost interest.
The task of building up with infinite patience and
resource his shattered party might not have excited
the enthusiasm of another man.   Disraeli was
touched with the romance of politics.   There was to
him a glamour in the ' Senate ' which not even the
boredom of drab demagogues could extinguish.   He
looked upon his life as an Arabian tale, and not even
fifty years, not even sixty, could drive from his mind
the coloured dreams of youth.   Fortunately, perhaps,
for himself success came to him grudgingly and with
slow foot.   It was not his fate in middle life to be
wearied with the care and dignity of high office.
When at last he became Prime Minister—when, in
his own phrase, he had ' climbed to the top of the greasy
pole '—he was in his sixty-fifth year, and yet could
combine with the tardy accomplishment of years all
the unrealised hopes of youth.

He had fought hard for his place ; he had overcome the obstacles thrown in his path by friends and
foes alike, and though he had won the battle, the
victory was still greeted with sneers by his opponents.
' A great triumph of intellect and courage and

patience and unscrupulousness,' said John Bright,
' employed in the service of a party full of prejudices
and selfishness, and wanting in brains.   The Tories
have hired Disraeli, and he has his reward from them.'
The silly jibe at the party ' wanting in brains '
should have seemed shameful even to the Radicals
of 1868, and John Bright, himself a mass of prejudice
and selfishness, was not the man to condemn those
sins in another.   The mere fact that John Bright
should have used these words proves how difficult
it is to kill a legend, and how bitterly the narrow-
minded, middle-class Radical has always hated the
romance and imagination which he can never share.

It was romance, then, which heartened Disraeli
for the strife, and which made him enjoy even the
solemn opposition of Gladstone.   Wherever he goes,
he still views life as a glittering pageant.   His letters
to Mrs. Brydges Williams, whom he addressed always
with a flattering candour, are vivid with the light-
hearted enthusiasm of youth.   ' The town is quite
mad,' he wrote in 1856 ;   ' fêtes and festivities night
and morn.   Never were there so many balls and
banquets.   No roof so hospitable this year as the Palace
itself.'   Wherever he went he gave proof of a like
joyousness.   He saw Paris in 1857 as the same gay
vision which smiled upon him in 1847, when Louis
Philippe was King and his friend.   ' Ten years, as
long as the siege of Troy, since I found myself last in
this place : Troy could not be more changed in the
time.   Everything squalid has been pulled down or

driven out of sight—a city of palaces and glittering streets, and illimitable parks and pleasure-grounds, statues and gondolas, and beautiful birds and deer. The Tuileries and the Louvre joined form a kingly residence worthy of Babylon.' The reception given to him and Mrs. Disraeli did not, he declared, turn their heads ; it tried their constitutions. They dined at the Tuileries, she by the Emperor, he by the side of the beautiful Empress. 'Round her swan-like neck,' thus he wrote, 'the Empress wore a necklace of emeralds and diamonds, such as might have been found in the cave of Aladdin ; and yet, though colossal gems, for her they were not too vast. After this I will tell you no more : the curtain should fall amid the brightest fire.'

And not only was he delighted at the pomp and ceremony of his life, not merely had he found in politics an excuse for the magnificence which suited his oriental temperament, but he saw in the changes and chances of foreign policy an absorbing drama. The adventures of his friends were episodes to them, to him were the enchantments of a golden world. When the Greeks offered the throne of Greece to Lord Stanley, he was dithyrambic in expectancy. 'If he accepts the change,' he wrote to Mrs. Brydges Williams, 'I shall lose a powerful friend and colleague. It is a dazzling adventure for the House of Stanley, but they are not an imaginative race, and I fancy they will prefer Knowsley to the Parthenon, and Lanca-shire to the " Attic plain ".' If only the throne had

M

been offered to Disraeli, who was more highly imaginative than the most of his race ! He would have accepted the crown as easily as he accepted the leadership of the House of Commons, and he would have worn it with a grace incomparable. Meanwhile, all was well with him. ' It is a privilege,' he wrote, ' to live in this age of rapid and brilliant events. What an error to consider it an utilitarian age ! It is one of infinite romance. Thrones tumble down and crowns are offered like a fairy tale, and the most powerful people in the world, male and female, a few years back were adventurers, exiles, and demireps. *Vive la bagatelle !* '

While he kept for the eyes of his friends these flowers of a luxuriant fancy, he wore in the general view an aspect of austerity. Though, as I have said, he arrived late, his arrival, even in the Palace, could be no longer deferred. Ever since he first went to the East in search of adventures, he had found himself at home in Courts. He had visited the Tuileries, the guest of a King and of an Emperor. In the Court of England, the country of his birth and service, he was still unhonoured. The early legend which had grown about his name had filled the minds of courtiers with suspicion, and Queen Victoria's early distrust of him had been vastly intensified by his attacks upon Sir Robert Peel. Little by little the barrier of misunderstanding was removed, partly by the tactful hand of the Prince Consort ; and, as is known to all, Disraeli became at last not merely the

Queen's favourite Minister, but her friend. The
confidence and friendship of his Sovereign, which for
many years Disraeli enjoyed, had their origin in the
sympathy which he expressed, with more than his
usual elaboration, at the death of Prince Albert.
That he should praise the Prince Consort in the
written and in the spoken word was but natural. A
tie of mutual admiration and respect had bound the
two men one to another. That which he said in
public was but a sincere echo of his private opinion.

'With Prince Albert,' he told Vitzthum, 'we have
buried our Sovereign. This German Prince has
governed England for twenty-one years with a wisdom
and energy such as none of our Kings has ever shown.
. . . If he had outlived some of our "old stagers,"
he would have given us, while retaining all constitutional guarantees, the blessings of absolute government. Of us younger men who are qualified to enter
the Cabinet, there is not one who would not willingly
have bowed to his experience.' The speech which
he made in the House applauded the services which
the Prince had rendered as 'the Prime Councillor of
a realm the political constitution of which did not
even recognise his political existence,' as well as the
encouragement to that culture in which the national
character had always been deficient. 'He was not
satisfied with detecting a want ; he resolved to supply
it.' In a letter in which he thanked Her Majesty
for a volume of the Prince's speeches, Disraeli's
eloquence took a bolder flight. He compared the

Prince with Sir Philip Sidney, and assured the Queen that he was the only person whom he had ever known to realise that ideal. 'There was in him,' wrote Disraeli, 'a union of the manly grace and sublime simplicity of chivalry with the intellectual splendour of the Attic Academe.' Well may Mr. Buckle call it a 'somewhat hyperbolic eulogium.' But there is not a word of it which was not sincerely felt and meant. It is but the coloured style which appears strange to an English eye.

At every mark of royal favour Disraeli was frankly delighted. When he and Mrs. Disraeli were given two of four places at the wedding of the Prince of Wales, he did not hide his satisfaction. 'There is no language,' he wrote, 'which can describe the rage, envy, and indignation of the great world. The Duchess of Marlboro' went into hysterics of mortification at the sight of my wife, who was on terms of considerable intimacy with her, and said it was really shameful, after the reception which the Duke had given the Prince of Wales at Blenheim ; and as for the Duchess of Manchester, who had been Mistress of the Robes in Lord Derby's Administration, she positively passed me for the season without recognition.' There the statesman speaks with the authentic voice of Disraeli the Younger, and proves that not even the stress of political controversy had extinguished the fire of his enthusiasm.

Even while he cried, *Vive la Bagatelle*, he pursued the profession of politics with tireless energy. In-

dustry is commonly accounted a dull virtue, and though
Disraeli was never dull, you cannot look back upon his
life without being impressed with the hard and solid
work which he accomplished.   Disraeli read blue-
books as other men read the newspaper.   He mastered
all the subjects on which he spoke in the House, by
sheer and unremitting industry.   If you read the
famous speech which he made upon the Indian
Mutiny, you might think that he had given all his life
to the study of Indian affairs.   When the Government
talked glibly, as Governments are wont to talk, about
the rebellion being ' well in hand,' and pretended that
it sent reinforcements to the East merely as a matter
of precaution, Disraeli knew and said better.   He
saw that the Indian people had long been waiting for
an occasion and a pretext.   The Russian War was
the occasion, and greased cartridges were the pretext.
They were a pretext only.   ' The rise and fall
of Empires,' he pointed out, ' are not affairs of
greased cartridges.   Such results are occasioned by
adequate causes and by an accumulation of adequate
causes.'

So that while he urged the suppression of the Mutiny
with a strong hand, while he promised the Government
all the support it needed, while he agreed to the
instant embodiment of the Militia, he would not close
the door of hope upon the Indian people.   It was not
enough to exact vengeance ;   justice should be
tempered with mercy ;   and the future of India should
be painted in brilliant colours.   And as if to show that

industry was no bar to an active imagination, he devised a large and ample settlement of peace. It was a scheme which he had already sketched in his youth, and of which he was destined many years later to produce the finished picture. 'The course,' said he, 'which I recommend is this : you ought at once, whether you receive news of success or defeat, to tell the people of India that the relation between them and their real ruler and Sovereign, Queen Victoria, shall be drawn nearer.' It was too much to ask of a Radical ministry that it should make any dream come true, nor did this dream turn to a reality for twenty years, and then it needed the magician's wand to call into being the Empire of the East. Nor has the magician's wisdom since stood in need of justification. What the Empress of India meant to our great dependency stands recorded in the page of history, and never did we have clearer evidence of Disraeli's foresight than when millions of Indians deplored the death of the Great White Queen, whom he had made a symbol of Empire and of clemency.

England always existed for Disraeli in close relationship with other countries. His view, which never wavered, was the view of a patriotic Englishman. Sir John Skelton, who met him when he visited Edinburgh in 1867, penetrated the ' Eastern mystery ' with a flash of good sense. 'They say, and say truly enough,' he wrote, ' what an actor the man is ! and yet the ultimate impression is of absolute sincerity and unreserve. Grant Duff will have it that he is an

alien. What 's England to him or he to England ?
There is just where they are wrong. Whig or Radical or Tory don't matter much perhaps ; but this
mightier Venice—this Imperial Republic on which
the sun never sets—that vision fascinates him, or I am
much mistaken. England is the Israel of his imagination, and he will be the Imperial Minister before he
dies—if he gets the chance.' He got the chance,
and justified most accurately the wise prophecy of
Sir John Skelton, who read Disraeli's character like
an open book, even in acknowledging that his ' face
was more like a mask than ever, and the division
between him and mere mortals more marked.' An
appreciation a dozen times better worth than the
fumbling malignity of disappointed Radicals.

Disraeli, then, was an Imperialist born out of due
time, and as he was a statesman of constructive imagination, he was determined, if he could, to convert his
ideas into realities. The key-note of his foreign policy
was, as I have said, an alliance with France. He
cared not who was head of the State, King or Emperor,
he would have him, if he could, England's friend. A
close intimacy with Napoleon iii. succeeded an intimacy
with Louis Philippe, and an old acquaintance persuaded Disraeli to treat Napoleon with an easier
familiarity. He had known him in the days when
he too was floating on the surface of English society
as a misunderstood adventurer. To-day he was on
a throne, and Disraeli aspired to the governance of
England. Again he would have said, *Vive la Baga-*

telle ! And he did not scruple to send an emissary
to the Court of the Tuileries. The emissary was
bidden to speak with a candour not often employed by
the subject of one State towards the monarch of
another. He discovered to Napoleon all the hopes
and fears of his chief. What Disraeli desired
before all things was that Napoleon should forget
the slights put upon him by maladroit Ministers,
and become frankly reconciled with the people of
England.

If Napoleon wished to increase his dominions,
Disraeli would not put any obstacles in his way. ' He
is an Emperor,' said he, with perfect truth, ' and should
have an Empire.' He was resolved that England
should not betray a paralysing nervousness at Napoleon's
activity upon the sea. He sketched for him the sort
of speech which he knew well would satisfy the susceptibilities of Englishmen. ' Let the Emperor take
an early opportunity,' he suggested, ' of referring to
the state of the French Navy ; let him allude with a
just pride to his efforts to restore the marine of France
to its ancient and proper force ; let him express his
surprise that it should be looked upon with jealousy
by the Power which he trusts will always prove the
ally of France ; that France seeks no undue supremacy
upon the sea.' Napoleon paid Disraeli the high compliment of taking his advice, and thus the two men laid
the foundations of an alliance which, shaken often,
has not yet been overthrown.

It was a great misfortune for England that Disraeli

had no share of the government during the fateful
years 1860-1864. The peace of the world was then
threatened in many quarters. There was trouble
in Poland ; the vexed questions which arose from the
Civil War in America perplexed our nerveless politicians. Finally, the events of Schleswig-Holstein
were preparing the way for the vast conflict which
presently tore the world asunder. And Lord John
Russell was our Foreign Minister ! His policy
was simple and dangerous. It was to intervene in
word, and to abstain from action. In every case in
which he meddled he ran the risk, incurred by the
fool who intervenes in a fight between man and wife,
of being attacked vigorously by both parties. Not
daring to come forth as the friend of any State, he
presumed to pester them all with advice, and made the
world our enemy. In these troubled times Disraeli
made mistakes—as who did not ?—but at least he
had a policy, and he did not grope vainly in the dark.
Before all things, he thought it inexpedient to interfere
in the domestic affairs of foreign nations. He
admitted, of course, that it was our imperative duty
to interfere where the interests or honour of our
country were at stake. But, said he, ' the general
principle that we ought not to interfere in the affairs of
foreign nations unless there is a clear necessity, and
that, generally speaking, it ought to be held a political
dogma that the people of other countries should settle
their own affairs without the intervention of foreign
influence or foreign power, is one which, I think, the

House does not only accept, but, I think, will cordially agree to.'

It was a dogma which in truth Lord John Russell did not accept. There was no question of foreign affairs in which Russell had not, at some stage, as Mr. Buckle truly says, 'usually with the active support of the Prime Minister, written strong despatches, or taken other steps calculated to lead to armed conflict, only to draw back afterwards, not always without humiliation, under pressure from the Court, or the Cabinet, or the Opposition, or the Country.' It was, as Disraeli called it, a policy of 'meddle and muddle,' and the Foreign Minister's weakness has not been without lamentable results in our day. At the same time it must be confessed that Disraeli did not divine the cause and purpose of Bismarck's adventure in Denmark. 'Prussia,' he thought, 'without nationality, the principle of the day, is clearly the subject for partition.' It would have been impossible to hazard a more foolish opinion, and there was the less excuse for it, because Bismarck had outlined his policy to Disraeli at a party at Brunnow's in 1862, in terms of the utmost candour. 'I shall soon be compelled,' he had said, 'to undertake the conduct of the Prussian Government. My first care will be to reorganise the army, with or without the Landtag. As soon as the army shall have been brought into such a condition as to inspire respect, I shall seize the first best pretext to declare war against Austria, dissolve the German Diet, subdue the minor States, and give national unity

to Germany under Prussian leadership.   I have come
here to say this to the Queen's Ministers.'   And
Disraeli talked about partition !

There is no episode in Disraeli's policy more
delicate than his treatment of the Church.   That
Disraeli had a firm faith in the Church of England
as a religious and political institution there is no doubt.
' There are few great things left in England,' he said,
' and the Church is one.'   And he defended the
Church with a far greater zeal than did Gladstone,
who was a bishop strayed into a wrong profession.
During his many years of opposition, Disraeli did his
best to strengthen the Church and to defend her from
the assaults of her enemies.   He opposed, and opposed
successfully, Sir John Trelawny's Bill for the abolition
of Church rates.   In his zeal for the Church he went
far beyond the discretion of Derby.   Above all, he
was a stout maintainer of orthodoxy.   Every mani-
festation of heresy, whether it came in the shape of
Essays and Reviews, or as specimens of German
theology, found in him a determined opponent.   He
was in favour of free inquiry on all subjects, but he
thought, with good reason, that ' free inquiry should
be made by free inquirers,' and that Jowett and Temple
' had entered into engagements with the people of this
country quite inconsistent with the views advanced in
their prolusions.'

His orthodoxy sprang, as Mr. Buckle acutely
points out, ' from a realisation of the utility of religion
to the civil magistrate, but also, it appears, from intel-

lectual conviction, and from a jealousy on behalf of
his own sacred race, the original recipients and trans-
mitters of religious truth.' It is the old and wayward
claim of Calvary as well as Sinai for the Jews. This
view exasperated, as well it might, many devout
Christians, and Disraeli clung to it with a frank
obstinacy. 'For myself,' he wrote in a letter addressed
to a clergyman, ' I look upon the Church as the only
Jewish institution that remains, and irrespective of its
being the depository of divine truth, must ever cling
to it as the visible means which embalms the memory
of my race, their deeds and thoughts, and connects
their blood with the origin of things.' If this is a
view which no Christian will accept, it explains in a
few lines, if it does not justify, Disraeli's sincere
devotion to the Church of England.

Nowhere did Disraeli appear with greater advantage
as the defender of the Church than in the Sheldonian
Theatre on 25th November 1864. He came to
Oxford at the invitation of Wilberforce, and he spoke
in favour of a society for endowing small livings. The
situation was one in which Disraeli took a natural
pleasure. To many it might have seemed a paradox
that he should address the dons and the country clergy
of England upon the doctrines of their religion. To
make the paradox still more evident, Disraeli wore a
velvet coat, as a sign that he was not wholly awake
to the gravity of the occasion. Assuredly what he
said must have puzzled his audience. In the very
stronghold of *Essays and Reviews* he dared to attack

the champions of the Broad Church. He could
understand how they might reject inspiration and
miracles. He could not understand how, having
arrived at these conclusions, they should remain
'sworn supporters of ecclesiastical establishments,
fervent upholders, or dignitaries of the Church.'

For himself, he refused to admit that the age of
faith had passed. Rather he thought that the characteristic of the present age was a craving credulity.
'Why, my Lord,' he exclaimed, 'man is a being born
to believe. And if no Church comes forward with
its title-deeds of truth, sustained by the tradition of
sacred ages and by the convictions of countless generations, to guide him, he will find altars and idols in his
own heart and imagination.' And so he turned to the
men of science, who were then beginning the period
of their tyranny, attacked the dogmatic evolutionists,
and set the contrast between their creed and the creed
of the Church in a single phrase. 'What is the
question,' he asked, 'now placed before society with a
glib assurance the most astounding ? The question
is this : Is man an ape or an angel ? My Lord, I am
on the side of the angels.' Disraeli, always a phrase-
maker, was never more happily inspired. The retort
upon science assured one-half of his audience and
mystified the other, and is not likely to fade from the
memory of man. It was also serious ; it expressed
in a few words Disraeli's deepest convictions : and
they were foolish who, misled by the velvet coat and a
nonchalant manner, thought that Disraeli was smiling

at his auditors. The truth is, that whatever Disraeli said and wrote about religion is all of a piece, and those who would discover what his mature views really were will find them reiterated with elaboration in a preface to his novels, written in 1870.

Among the questions of domestic policy which then disturbed the minds of men parliamentary reform takes a foremost place. Reform is a subject of some dulness, and of great danger. No Reform Bill has ever been passed which was not a leap in the dark, a leap, moreover, which has always carried us into the pit. Whatever safeguards are put into a Bill are presently nullified, and that which is granted as a privilege ends by being looked upon as a right. Unhappily he who sets a ball rolling down the hill has no power to stop it, and England still suffers from what was the logical outcome of the Bill which Disraeli passed in 1867. It is curious to note that in those days the word ' democratic ' was, as it should always be, a term of reproach. To-day it is a word of fulsome flattery. Lord Shaftesbury cannot be described as a reactionary, and this is what he wrote to Disraeli in 1865 : ' You will not, I hope, be offended that I presume to thank you for your speech on the Baines Bill. The sentiments and the language were worthy of each other, and a masterly protest against any truckling to democracy. I believe that in proportion as a man is a deep, sincere, and consistent lover of *social*, civil, and religious liberty, he will be a deep, sincere, and consistent hater of pure democracy, as adverse to all three.' That is perfectly true. We know to-day that democracy is the bitter, irreconcilable foe of freedom. Disraeli too knew it, and in his optimism thought that he could stay the ball set rolling down the hill when he would. He regarded his own Franchise Bill as popular and not democratic ; and so it might have proved, had it not led to others. The truth is that when you once start upon the road of reform you seek finality in vain. No safeguards are strong enough to hold back the incoming tide of democracy, and all moderate Bills are swept away by the turbid waves of manhood suffrage. Disraeli's measure was designed to be very 'popular.' Its outcome is that to-day the rich pay and the poor govern, a condition of things which must involve even the greatest State in ruin.

Nevertheless, Disraeli was quite right when he claimed that reform was no monopoly of the Whigs. Both parties have gambled with the votes of the people, and must share the blame for the degradation of England. But, having said what must be said in dispraise, we cannot but admire the zeal wherewith Disraeli attempted to reduce the inherent dangers of his measure, and the skill with which he carried it to a triumphant end. His passage of the bill was a marvel of tactics. At last he met Gladstone, his natural foe, in single combat, and routed him utterly. He attacked his new adversary as he had attacked Peel, his old adversary, with the flaunts and jibes against which fate has made no armour. The victory of Disraeli and of the party was hailed everywhere as crushing and complete. Corry told him that his fame was in the mouth of every labourer. ' My private opinion,' said he, ' is that of my aunt's carpenter, who "having heard say that Mr. Disraeli had laid Mr. Gladstone on his back," thinks that you really knocked that godly man down. I have too much jealousy for your fair fame to undeceive him.'

Thus the carpenter ; and at the higher end of the scale Count Vitzthum was loud in approval. His tribute, weighed and balanced, is worth citing, as the expression of a mature and detached judgment. ' I never regretted my absence from England so much,' he wrote. ' I need not to tell you the joy I felt at your victory. I was sure of it. May I tell you frankly why ? Looking on, without party bias, during fourteen years, I could not help being struck by the fact that you appeared the only man in England working for posterity. Your genius bore, to my eyes, always the historical stamp, and I never listened to a speech of yours without thinking—this word, this sentence, will be remembered a hundred years hence.' Thus Vitzthum anticipated posterity ; and time is fast proving the soundness of his opinion. Disraeli's success in the House of Commons did more than evoke the praises of his friends. It made him Prime Minister of England. Thus to the equal applause of counts and carpenters he climbed the greasy pole.

V.—THE END

As Mr. Buckle neared the end of his work, his
hero increased in interest, and the biographer rose
always with the occasion.   His method of allowing
the actors in the political drama, which it has been his
good fortune to conduct, to tell their own story in
their own words, admirably justified itself.   Where
the interlocutors speak with elegance and authority,
the more we are given of their own authentic speech
the better.   And how shall a play ever slacken its
hold upon us, in which Queen Victoria and Disraeli
are cast for the chief parts, and in which Lord Salisbury,
Gortschakoff, and Bismarck are permitted to speak a
line now and again ?

Mr. Buckle, then, squandered none of the wealth
of material that was given him.   He knew well how
to expend it to the best purpose.   In 1867, Disraeli,
flushed with the victory of the Reform Bill, was conscious of the reaction which often follows victory, and
cherished no illusion of an immediate triumph.   Few
statesmen, as I have said, have reached their final glory
with greater hardship than he.   He was nearing seventy
when for the first time he was assured the strength and
the time to make the dreams, which he had dreamed for
England, realities.   He had little reason to repine or
complain.   He had justified his boyish boast that when
he raised his voice in the House of Commons a dropped
pin might be heard.   And yet he could not but stifle
one regret.   No man ever had a firmer faith in Youth

N

than he. The eloquent hymn which he sang in
Coningsby to Youth and its manifold achievements
still echoed in his ears, as it echoes in ours ; and the
privilege of action, supported and uncontrolled, was
not his until he had reached the allotted span of life.
' Power ! ' said he in the hour of his triumph, ' it has
come to me too late. There were days when on
waking I felt I could move dynasties and governments,
but that has passed away.' It had not passed away, as
Disraeli was destined presently to show. When once
the battle was engaged, he found that neither years
nor disease had destroyed the faculty of action that was
in him.

Disraeli, being a man of imagination, delighted
in the unexpected, and he was not unwilling to
find in his own career an element of surprise.
Well enough he knew, when he was sincere and
by himself, that there was no surprise in his career.
What he had gained he had worked for with a conscious determination. Though it suited his enemies
to declare that he was no better than a Jewish
trickster, a mere conjurer, who could keep six balls
revolving in the air, the abuse was so obviously irrelevant that it missed its mark. Disraeli had prepared
himself for the leadership of his party by years of hard
and patient toil. There is only one short cut to
political success—the short cut, which Gladstone
took, of exciting the baser passions of the ignorant.
Disraeli was never a demagogue. He never stooped
to the people. He based the opinions, which he held

loyally and strenuously, upon a wide knowledge of
the past ; and if these opinions were accepted by
the people, he was prepared to lead it, as long as it
would follow him.   He scorned always to give himself the title of leader, as others claimed it, when they
were following only the baaing of the sheep.

It was not for him to stump the country, to bombard
Midlothian with garrulity, to invent atrocities. ' I
have never in the course of my life,' he once said with
perfect truth, ' obtruded myself on any meeting of my
fellow-countrymen unless I was locally connected
with them, or there were peculiar circumstances
which might vindicate me from the imputation of
thrusting myself unnecessarily on their attention.'
He was, in brief, endowed with the aristocracy of
genius, and was not of those whom any man might
approach with impunity.   Because he served England,
he knew no reason why the first comer should accost
him.   I saw him but once in my boyhood, and recognised in him instantly the complete antithesis of
Gladstone.   It was on the platform at Swindon, and
Disraeli (he was then Lord Beaconsfield) paced up
and down on Lord Rowton's arm, waiting for a train.
As he thus paced, slowly and wearily, a bluff and hearty
bagman assailed him in the best of humours. ' I
have always voted for your side, Lord Beaconsfield,'
said the bagman, ' and I should like to take you by the
hand.'   Beaconsfield lifted his eyes for an instant and
shook his head. ' I do not know you,' said he, and
resumed his walk.   Had so happy an encounter come

to Mr. Gladstone, what would he not have done ?
He would have taken his assailant by both hands, and
asked him to keep his umbrella as a souvenir.

Disraeli, being no demagogue, said what he thought,
not what he hoped would be acceptable.   Nothing is
more clearly evident in the speeches of these later
years than the sound sense and quick prescience which
inform them.   Disraeli had the true gift of the statesman : he could infer what would be from what had
been ; he could look into the future with the wise eyes
of the past.   Always happy in phrase and aphorism,
he knew better than any other how to force his meaning upon his audience and to make it linger in its
memory.   The flouts and gibes of which he was
so easy a master were (so to say) the light horse in his
attack.   When (in 1872) he made his celebrated
speech at Manchester, in which he coined the now
famous phrase, *Sanitas sanitatum, omnia sanitas,* and
declared that 'after all, the first consideration of a
Minister should be the health of a people,' he would
not have produced his due effect unless he had pictured
his adversaries in a passage that is never likely to be
forgotten.   'As I sat opposite the Treasury Bench,'
said he, 'the Ministers reminded me of one of those
marine landscapes not very unusual on the coasts of
South America.   You behold a range of exhausted
volcanoes.   Not a flame flickers on a single pallid
crest.   But the situation is still dangerous.   There are
occasional earthquakes, and ever and anon the dark
rumbling of the sea.'   Here there is not a word

awry.   The precise effect which the orator intended is produced without fuss or trouble, and you wonder that the exhausted volcanoes ever again dared to raise their pallid crests upon the Treasury Bench.

Turn where you will in the speeches of his later years, and you will find admirable specimens of Disraeli's eloquent wisdom.   The sure test of his wisdom is that what he said half a century ago is as true to-day as on the day whereon it was spoken.   Let me take at random a few specimens, which will explain Disraeli's quick perception and lucid utterance more clearly than pages of commentary.   Here, for instance, is a sketch of the Irish character, made in 1868 on the hustings at Aylesbury, which has lost nothing of its truth.   'The Irishman,' said Disraeli, ' is an imaginative being.   He lives on an island in a damp climate, and contiguous to the melancholy ocean.   There is no nation that leads so monotonous a life as the Irish, because their only occupation is the cultivation of the soil before them.   These men are discontented because they are not amused.   The Irishman in other countries, when he has a fair field for his talents in various occupations, is equal, if not superior, to most races ; and it is not the fault of the Government that there is not that variety of occupation in Ireland.   I may say with frankness that I think it is the fault of the Irish.   If they led that kind of life which would invite the introduction of capital into the country, all this ability might be utilised ; and instead of those feelings which they acquire by brooding

over the history of their country, a great part of which
is merely traditionary, you would find men acquiring
fortunes and arriving at conclusions in politics entirely
different from those which they now offer.'   There
we have the plain sense of the Irish question.   And
had Disraeli's good counsel been followed, had Gladstone and others not found it profitable to appeal to a
false sentimentality, there might to-day be no Irish
question at all.

With the same cold eye of understanding wherewith he envisaged Ireland, Disraeli envisaged
America also.   He was not afraid to call the
poker player's bluff, and had our governors always
showed his courage, we should not have lost so
many games.   He pointed out that it was only
to Great Britain that the Americans were insolent
and offensive, and they were insolent and offensive to
us because they believed that they could adopt this
attitude with impunity.   And here is the warning
that he gave : 'The danger is this—they habitually
excite the passions of millions, and some unfortunate
thing happens, or some unfortunate thing is said in
either country ; the fire lights up, it is beyond their
control, and the two nations are landed in a contest
which they can no longer control or prevent.   Though
I should look upon it as the darkest hour of my life
were I to counsel or even support in this House a war
with the United States, still the United States should
know that they are not an exception to the other
countries of the world ; that we do not permit

ourselves to be insulted by any other country in the
world, and that they cannot be an exception.' Thus
Disraeli ; and still our Ministers, when England is
assaulted by the rowdy rhetoric of America, hasten to
offer whatever appeasement they may, and have even
legislated in Ireland with an eye and an ear resolutely
fixed upon an inimical Washington.

Disraeli, however, was never content with short
views. He was gifted with prescience and imagination.
Ideas had no terror for him. And he prepared to-day
for what he surely knew would come about to-morrow.
No one of his time, as I have said, had a clearer vision
than he of what would be the future of our Colonial
Empire ; and on the strength of a hasty word spoken
in jest to Lord Malmesbury he has been accused by
his enemies of despising our oversea dominions. I
have already quoted what he thought our Colonial
policy should be in 1850 and 1851. Now hear what
he said in the memorable speech made at the Crystal
Palace in 1872, a speech in which he advocated already
an imperial tariff, securities for the people of England
for the enjoyment of the unappropriated lands which
belonged to the Sovereign as their trustee, and a military
code which should have precisely defined the means
and responsibilities by which the colonies should be
defended and by which the mother country should call
for aid from the colonies themselves.

' Well,' asked he, ' what has been the result of this
attempt during the reign of Liberalism for the disinte-
gration of the Empire ? It has entirely failed. But how

has it failed ?   Through the sympathy of the colonies
for the mother country.   They have decided that the
Empire shall not be destroyed ; and in my opinion no
Minister in this country will do his duty who neglects
any opportunity of reconstructing as much as possible
our Colonial Empire, and of responding to those
distant sympathies which may become the source of
incalculable strength and happiness to this land.'   As
Disraeli forecast it, so has it been, and events have
again and again proved the truth of that which was
spoken in 1872.   Therein, indeed, lies the value of
Disraeli's career and its ample record.   They reveal
to us a body of Tory doctrine which it is still a stern
duty to ponder and expound.

The political game, as it is played in England, bears
this resemblance to the game of fives, that you must
get your adversary out before you may begin to score
yourself.   And during the last quarter-century of his
life, Disraeli was faced by an adversary whom he could
not ignore, and whom he could not meet with the
good humour which he gladly showed to Hartington
and Granville.   His dislike and distrust of Gladstone
were again and again loudly expressed, and Gladstone
reciprocated the dislike and distrust with all his own
bitterness.   On either side the antipathy was natural
and unconquerable.   In Disraeli's eyes Gladstone was
a malignant Tartuffe, dominated by hypocrisy and
malice.   To Sir Stafford Northcote Disraeli complained of Gladstone's 'vindictiveness,' which, said
he, was a great fault in the leader of a party, who

ought to be above personal feelings. ' This will be
" nuts " to Gladstone,' he wrote, when the harvest
failed in 1880, ' who will never rest till he has destroyed the landed interest. If he were younger the
Crown would be in peril.' [1] Above all, he had a
profound contempt for Gladstone's writings. Though
he is himself at times sadly at fault, what he admired
in others was style. ' In letters,' he wrote to Lady
Bradford in 1875, ' the first, and greatest, condition
of success is—style. It is that by which the great
authors live.' And he found in the works of Gladstone everything that seemed to him to be vicious. ' I
think his usual style,' said he, ' the worst I know of
any public man ; and that it is marvellous how so
consummate an orator should, the moment he takes
his pen, be so involved, cumbersome, and infelicitous
in expression.' Had Disraeli lived to read Gladstone's
printed speeches he would have included them in the
same condemnation, since they have been found
unintelligible even to his most ardent admirers. But
Disraeli, like the rest, had fallen under the histrion's
sway, and, deceived by the flashing eye and shaking
voice, had thought his great adversary's oratory better
than it was.

Here, then, is a definite difference between the two
men. Disraeli was a man of letters who never wrote

[1] If you could measure the difference between the two men,
read the letters which passed between them in 1858, when Disraeli magnanimously urged Gladstone to rejoin the Conservative
Party. There is no doubt which of them had the advantage in
generosity and good manners.

a note without thinking about the turn of the phrase. Gladstone, with all his love of books, was wholly insensitive to the claim of style. He poured out his confused thoughts upon paper in confused words. The few years which have passed since his death have wholly obliterated his writings from the minds of men. What he wrote in his lifetime was read by those fanatical persons who believed him to be a saviour of the country, and who regarded him not as a man of letters but as an inspired prophet. Now that all the world knows that he was no prophet, the world has lost interest in his theology, in his criticism, in his mixed thoughts about Homer. Meanwhile the fame of Disraeli, the writer, has steadily increased. His novels are better understood, and more fairly judged for good and evil to-day than ever they were, and they have found a permanent place in the literature of their time. Here is a fine reversal of opinion ! And it is satisfactory to think that in so brief a span of years effective justice has been done.

Indeed, by a strange perversion of the truth, the two men were in their lifetime put in their wrong places. 'One of the most grievous and constant puzzles of King David,' said an ironist in the *Pall Mall Gazette* on 3rd March 1868, quoted by Mr. Buckle, ' was the prosperity of the wicked and scornful; and the same tremendous moral enigma has come down to our own days. . . . Like the Psalmist, the Liberal leader may well protest that verily he has cleansed his heart in vain and washed his hands in innocency ;

. . . as blamelessly as any curate he has written about *Ecce Homo* ; and he has never made a speech, even in the smallest country town, without calling out with David, " How foolish am I, and how ignorant ! " For all this, what does he see ? ' He saw the scorner who shot out the lip honoured among the people, and it was enough, as the ironist says, ' to make an honest man rend his mantle and shave his head and sit down among the ashes inconsolable.'

Again the two men have (so to say) changed their reputations. The idle apprentice, Disraeli, has become in the eyes of the present generation the industrious. He was called a Jew trickster, and to-day we know so much about him, thanks to his biographers, that henceforth none will doubt his sincerity. While Gladstone grasped eagerly at the opinions of others, hoping that his acceptance of them might bring him votes, Disraeli fashioned his own opinions and never stooped, as I have said, to the methods of the demagogue. We know now that it was the tortuous mind of Gladstone that was fertile in trickery, that the man who could deceive himself had no difficulty in deceiving others. Disraeli could never have stooped to the ingenious excuses which Gladstone thought were good enough to bamboozle the world withal. He could not have escaped from a promise to put a certain measure in the forefront of his policy by declaring that the forefront was a line and not a point. Surely in the matter of political morality there is no comparison between the two men.　Time and knowledge have proved the advantage to be all on the side of Disraeli.

Through many years of fluent garrulity the Radicals have taunted Disraeli with a carelessness about the truth.　They have held up their own Gladstone as a pure model of veracity.　The evidence which they bring forward is insufficient, and coloured by their own peculiar temperament.　Disraeli, a natural courtier, did not despise the little arts by which pleasure is given to others and no harm is done.　Mr. Buckle cites an admirable example of his craft in this kind.　'A well-known and delightful lady'—it is Mr. G. W. E. Russell who tells the story—tried to make him read *The New Republic*, and write a favourable word about it for the author's encouragement. He replied : " I am not as strong as I was, and I cannot undertake to read your young friend's romances; but give me a sheet of paper."　So then and there he sate down and wrote : " Dear Mrs. S——, I am sorry I cannot dine with you next week, but I shall be at Hughenden.　Would that my solitude could be peopled with the bright creations of Mr. Mallock's fancy."'　As Mr. Russell says, 'bright creations' as an epitome of a book which he had not read is a stroke of genius.　No doubt the phrase was flattering to Mr. Mallock, and the underlying inaccuracy is easily pardoned.　I have seen this simple anecdote seized upon as a proof of Disraeli's faslehood, and no doubt it will bring comfort to many a Radical breast. And then I remember what Mr. Gladstone said when

he had unjustly accused Colonel Dopping of feloni-
ously using a rifle. ' I did not say that the rifle was
loaded,' he objected, and thought himself an injured
man. That he had libelled a gallant soldier mattered
not to him. The glib excuse was ready upon his
tongue. And there is no uncertainty which of the
men put a better, more liberal interpretation upon the
truth.

As in political thought, so in political oratory the
advantage is with Disraeli. Master as he was of
satire, especially in the brilliant days of his attack upon
Peel, he was always the closest of reasoners : he based
his arguments upon wisely collected and indestructible
facts. In his style of speaking he was an artist always,
and he had the artist's economy of words. There is
no cotton-wool in the texture of his speech. All is
reduced to its lowest terms, and there is little doubt
about the meaning. The orator does not attempt to
cover up the confusion of his mind by a mass of words.
His periods are clear-cut and sustained. When you
put down a speech of Disraeli's you know precisely
what he has thought and said ; its effect is made permanent upon your mind by a quick jest or happy
aphorism ; and over the whole flickers a lambent
flame of wit and humour. The result is that the
speeches of Disraeli have lost none of their force with
the years. They are among the few specimens which
remain to us of breathing, living oratory.

What a contrast is afforded us by the speeches of
Gladstone ! The best of them make us wonder that

the two men were ever held to be rivals. Gladstone's torrent of eloquence is impetuous and undammed. It rushes along swift and purposeless, like a stream that has escaped from its banks. The Radical orator kept as little control upon his words as upon his thoughts, and his speeches are already almost unintelligible. He gives you a vague impression of nobility, humility, self-sacrifice—in brief, of all the virtues coarsely blent together ; and when you attempt to check the impression, you find that all the while you have been the victim of a mystification. Moreover, Gladstone could not, even if he would, touch the reasoning faculty of his hearers. He appeals always to passion or emotion, and seems as though he expected by the mere act of saying nothing definite to catch the innocent off their guard. He hopes to communicate to others the inebriation caused him by his own verbosity, and he hopes in vain. Such were the two men who fought for the right to govern England, and it is fortunate for England that in the critical years between 1874 and 1880 genius got the better of talent.

For that is the essential difference between the two men : Disraeli was a man of genius. Gladstone was forced to make the best of the talent entrusted to him. Genius, if it be hard to define, is easy to detect. Assuredly it is not synonymous with ' taking pains,' as has been foolishly supposed. Rather it is the quick faculty of thinking, writing, and acting spontaneously and without drudgery. The man of genius, of course, cannot achieve his aim without taking pains ; but the possession of the rarest gift of all enables him (so to say) to leave out the intermediate steps between conception and fruition.   He strikes off at a blow that which industrious talent vainly attempts to accomplish by hard toil.   And not only does the man of genius work by another method ; he arrives at a result beyond the reach of industrious talent.   What he does and says has a supreme and lasting quality of its own. He attaches succeeding generations more easily than he can attach his own.   The very freshness of his attack baffles his contemporaries, and compels him to conquer his public before he can enthral it.   Often the balance is not redressed until after his death.   And it is on the vital distinction between genius and talent which has ensured to Disraeli a growing fame, while the bays which once encircled the Olympian brow of Gladstone are already withered and cast away.

Disraeli was a sojourner in a strange land, an alien who aspired to the governance of what was to him and to his race a foreign country.   And he aspired not in vain, precisely because he was a man of genius.   For genius transcends the boundaries and frontiers of race, and makes its happy possessor an understanding citizen in whatever state he inhabits. Now, genius is rarely found among the Jews, who, appreciative of the works of others, and often good executants, are seldom artists or capable of creative work.   Above all, they may rarely be trusted with the work of governing.   Having no country of their own, they seldom comprehend the meaning of the word 'patriotism,' and they remain all the world over a dangerous *imperium in imperio*, finding their friends not in the country of their adoption, but wherever abroad Jewry is most strongly entrenched. For this reason it would be well if by a common rule Jews were excluded from the privilege of government. Their international minds prevent them from loyal service, and the habit of centuries compels them to convert all policies into the terms of money.

Wherever their influence is felt it is a sinister influence, and hidden underground. In truth, we can never hope to be well and loyally governed until we exclude Jews from our national councils. And then comes along the man of genius, not to invalidate an honest rule, but to show that only in a thousand years may it be broken with impunity. Disraeli is the one single Jew in our annals who has justified the public confidence reposed in him. A Jew by blood, and proud of what he believed to be an ancient race, he was in sympathy and temper wholly English. His patriotism, ever aflame, was the patriotism not of the Ghetto but of Great Britain. The rare gift of genius enabled him to understand the English aristocracy, among which he lived and upon which he relied for support. He advanced no Jews to places in his Cabinets. He knew but one end—the prosperity of Great Britain, and he worked for that end with an untiring loyalty. From beginning to end he fought a hard fight, in what he held to be the cause of England, against factious opposition and ill-health. In all the

admirable letters which he wrote to Queen Victoria
and to Lady Bradford, you will not find a single Jewish
touch.   In every line of his correspondence there
speaks an English Tory : as you read you marvel at
what genius may accomplish.   And even while
thanking God for the gift of Benjamin Disraeli, you
do not relent against the others of his race.   The
miracle that happened once is not likely to be repeated.

As Disraeli rigidly excluded the men of his own race
from the task of governing England, so he separated
himself from his people by an honest contempt of
money.   Until, in 1862, Andrew Montagu, a Yorkshire squire, came to his aid and took over his mort-
gages, he had been in the hands of money-lenders.
Probably these unhappy transactions afforded him a
deeper insight into the Jewish character than he had
gained elsewhere.   Throughout his long career he
had depended upon his own exertions for the wealth
that was necessary to support the dignity of his office.
And not even his malignant opponents at home—and
they were many—ever breathed a hint of corruption.
It was reserved for a Russian print, the *Golos*, in 1876,
to charge Lord Beaconsfield with having amassed a
fortune, in conjunction with the firm of Erlanger,
by speculating on the Eastern Question.   Schouva-
loff called upon him, as well he might, ' with a message
of horror and indignation ' ; and Rose, who had known
all there was to know of Disraeli's affairs for thirty
years, took the opportunity of protesting indignantly
to Corry.   ' If ever a man lived,' said he, ' who was

pure as snow in money matters, and more scrupulous than any living man in everything that concerned his pecuniary interests, it is Lord Beaconsfield, as history will show.' History has shown it already, and the high-mindedness of Lord Beaconsfield throws into a deep relief the carelessness of some of his successors.

Disraeli, then, was a Jew who had triumphed over Jewry, and who may not be taken as an example to the others of his race, between whom and him genius has set up an unscaleable fence. Throughout the years of his supremacy, and they were all too few, he worked day and night to place Great Britain in a dominating position. He was a brave man, who did not fear war in the last resort. He was also a wise man, who knew that war, whatever its issue, was the heaviest misfortune that can overtake a country. Once upon a time, when a rupture with Russia seemed imminent, Frederick Greenwood called upon him and found him in tears. But, being a man of action, he did not shrink from emergencies, and during his last and triumphant Ministry he set England upon a higher pinnacle of strength and dignity than she had mounted for many a year.

He had waited for power, and when it came it was complete and unquestioned. On the one hand he gained the whole-hearted confidence of the Queen ; on the other, he governed his devoted Cabinet without difficulty. The final responsibility of whatever was done at home and abroad he gladly assumed, and yet, like all great men, he knew how to depute work and let his colleagues have full scope. At the outset of his great term of office he devoted himself to domestic legislation, and gave practical shape to many of the ideas which he and his friends had cherished in the days of Young England, still an active influence with him. It is his foreign policy upon which his ultimate fame as a statesman rests, and it may be said that he met the great diplomatists of Europe on their chosen ground and conquered them. A Foreign Minister who faced Bismarck with composure, and who won from the Iron Chancellor not merely respect but friendship, has proved to the world both his candour and his courage.

Through the years in which Russia was striving to dominate Eastern Europe, Disraeli's difficult task was rendered yet more difficult, because he had to harmonise as best he could the high-hearted patriotism of Queen Victoria with Derby's cold and fish-like indifference. That the harmony remained unbroken until near the end was due to Disraeli's untiring tact. He succeeded in keeping Great Britain out of war, and won a bloodless victory over Russia at the Congress of Berlin. That, indeed, was the highest point of his career—a triumph that was worth all the weary years of waiting. From the very outset it was he who aroused the liveliest curiosity. He was the centre of the Congress, at which he carried by far the greatest weight of authority. ' Der alte Jude, das ist der Mann,' said Bismarck, and thus gave the key to the others. The truth is that Disraeli knew what he wanted, and had the courage to insist upon getting it. In nothing did he fail ; at no point did he condescend to compromise. With the greatest care had he laid his plans. Austria and Turkey were already on his side. His intentions were well known to Russia. Only the policy of Germany was uncertain, and what that was to be was speedily settled in amicable talk between Bismarck and Disraeli. The division of Bulgaria into two provinces, of which the northern province should have political autonomy, while the southern should remain as a portion of Turkey, with a measure of self-government, had been duly accepted by Russia. But Russia had insisted upon submitting to the Congress the British contention that the Sultan should have full military rights in the southern province, and especially the right to canton troops on its frontiers.

Disraeli was obdurate. He presented as an ulti-matum that which he had agreed to submit to the Congress. He was determined not to cede an inch to Russia ; and Bismarck, when, after a long even-ing's talk with him, discovered that he meant business, went gladly over to his side. While Russia hesitated, Disraeli prepared to leave Berlin, and ordered his special train to be got ready. A break-up of the Congress meant war between England and Russia, and Gortchakoff at last gave in. It was a triumph for Disraeli, and Bismarck did not hide his admira-tion of his rival, whom he rated far higher than Gortchakoff, Andrassy, and the rest. ' It was easy to transact business with him,' said he ; ' in a quarter of an hour you knew exactly how you stood with him ; the limits to which he was prepared to go were clearly defined, and a rapid summary soon precised matters.'

Thus the ambitions of Russia were foiled, and Cyprus, of whose acquisition Disraeli had dreamed in *Tancred*, became ours ; and the statesman who had manfully supported the dignity of Great Britain, returned in triumph, bearing with him ' Peace with Honour.' It was a fitting end of a great career. Distinctions were showered upon him. He received the Garter, and refused a Dukedom. Congratulations came to him from all sides and all parties. He survived the Congress three years, but his work was done. What could the rest be but an anti-climax ? He died on 19th April 1881, full of years, and in the proud consciousness that he had achieved much that he had set out to achieve.

No man of his age had a more fortunate career. He lived not one, but many lives. He fulfilled his destiny as a statesman and as a man of letters. Whatever he had touched had prospered under his hand. He had enjoyed the trust and affection of his Sovereign as no other statesman in England has ever enjoyed them. He had conquered English Society in his youth, and had retained his conquest, until in his age he became, as it were, the arbiter of the great world. His reputation stood as high on the Continent of Europe as it stood at home, and he had risen to the dominant place in Great Britain without ever truckling

to the folly, the ignorance, and the passion of the mob.
Throughout his life he won with equal ease the
friendship of men and women.   The letters which he
wrote to Lady Bradford and Lady Chesterfield are
an eloquent testimony to the esteem and affection in
which these ladies held him.   Such relationships,
indeed, are rare in the history of mankind, and happy
is he to whom they are given.   His wife, the constant
friend and companion of his life, watched with eager
sympathy his rise to power and influence, and died in
the fulness of her age.   Why, then, does Mr. Buckle
call his life ' at once a romance and a tragedy ' ?   Truly
it was a romance, because Disraeli, being of a romantic
temper, turned into romance whatever he did and
thought.   As he says himself, his heart remained
always young ; and he never lost his zest for the colour
and splendour of life, which are the real elements of
romance.   But tragedy ?   In vain we seek for it,
as in vain we seek for the mystery in which Disraeli
is said to have been enwrapped.   Mr. Monypenny
said that ' unless the mystery remained when he had
finished his labours, he would have failed in his task
of portraiture.'   Neither he nor Mr. Buckle has
failed in his task, and whatever mystery ever existed—
if indeed any mystery existed—is dispelled.   A simpler
career, more plainly sketched and more successfully
followed to the end, I do not know.   Disraeli was
candid to himself and to his friends, and the mass of
material, piously gathered by his biographers and skil-
fully displayed, leaves neither his motives nor his

actions in doubt.   But the world, if it may not have a
mystery, will cling to a paradox, and will still pretend
to believe that the one man of his time, who had both
the faculty and the will to reveal the secrets of his
soul, is enwrapped in an impenetrable veil, which
knowledge and clairvoyance are alike incapable of
tearing asunder.

VI.—THE NOVELS

The success, which was won by Disraeli's novels
in the writer's own lifetime, was perforce a success
of scandal.   It was far beyond the wit of partisans
to distinguish the novelist from the fighting politician, and prejudiced readers allowed their judgment
of fiction to be confused by the passions of the
hustings.   Thus, as the Whig dogs have always been
permitted to dictate to Englishmen what they should
think, the novels of Disraeli were naturally misunderstood.   They have been considered a mere part of
his political career, and condemned as worthless by
excited politicians.   A biography, published as early
as 1854, put them in what its author thought their
place.   Another and a shameful biography, now, I
believe, withdrawn from the press, used them for an
excuse of insolent vituperation.   The political passions
of sixty years ago have grown cool with age, and at
last Disraeli, the Novelist, is judged by his merits, and
is set far higher among the writers of fiction than even
he dared to hope.

His novels and tales are more widely read to-day and more highly appreciated than ever they were. He fights for esteem with Dickens and Thackeray, and issues not wholly worsted from the encounter. Upon what then does his mastery rest ? By what power do *Coningsby* and *Sybil* keep their hold upon our imaginations ? We shall find it easier to answer these questions if we define clearly the limitations of his genius. To begin with, there is the paradox of his style. If ever a man of letters came into this world with his calling fixed upon him, it was Benjamin Disraeli. As he said himself, he was born in a library, the son of an accomplished and erudite writer. His early models were Lucian and Voltaire, and he proved himself not unworthy of them. *The Infernal Marriage* and *Ixion in Heaven* are written in a measured style and with a restraint of wit, which suggest that, had he chosen to castigate his talent, he might have taken a place among the great ironists. The admirable *Popanilla*, an earlier work than these two little masterpieces, challenges in youthful confidence a comparison with Swift. In an interval between *Popanilla* and *The Infernal Marriage*, Disraeli had discovered a gift of rhetoric, which presently obliterated the good example of Lucian and Voltaire from his mind. Instead, he took for his models Byron and Goethe, and expressed all the extravagance of his Eastern mind in a kind of poetic prose or prose poetry. In *Contarini Fleming* he showed the insensitiveness of his ear by writing what follows :

> Food or water have they none,
> No genial fount, no graceful tree
> Rise with their pleasant company,
> Never a beast or bird is there,
> In that hoary desert bare.
> Nothing breaks the almighty stillness.
> Even the jackal's felon cry
> Might seem a soothing melody.

Disraeli printed these lines as prose, and believed them prose. I have broken them up into lines, and given them, I think, their proper aspect.

As Disraeli could not distinguish clearly between prose and verse, so he did not trouble to understand the structure of the English sentence. He soon separated himself from the knowledge of grammar, which once seemed instinctive in him. With a sublime carelessness he broke all the rules. He liked not to leave his relatives unaccompanied by an ' and.' He could write sentences such as ' resolute and reckless, nothing deterred Villebecque.' He delighted in wholly inexpressive words, and in large phrases of meaningless exaggeration. He talks at large about Palladian piles and Gothic edifices. His description of houses and places leaves them unrecognisable. He attempts to excite your wonder by ' pictures, which are the envy of the collector,' by ' Limoges enamels the despair of the dilettante.' The No-man's Land in Paris, inhabited by Sidonia, is a sheer nightmare, as confusedly exotic as its exotic owner. What are we to think of such a hall as this : ' The roof was carved and gilt in the honeycomb style prevalent in the Saracenic buildings ; the walls were hung with leather stamped in rich and vivid patterns ; the floor was a flood of mosaic ; about were statues of negroes of human size, with faces of wild expression, and holding in their outstretched hands silver torches that blazed with an almost painful brilliancy ' ? It would be difficult, indeed, to match this orgie of colour and design.

The orgie means nothing more than that Disraeli's love of magnificence outran his taste. He was the true child of his age in his hatred of simplicity. He mixed all the styles with a careless profusion, and he thought that there was no more to be said by way of praise when a ' saloon ' had been ' decorated in encaustic by the most celebrated artists of Munich.' Leslie Stephen has found the simplest explanation of this extravagance, which is also the truest. ' Disraeli,' he writes, ' had a real unfeigned delight in simple splendour, in " ropes of pearls," in priceless diamonds, gorgeous clothing, and magnificent furniture.' And he defends the delight with justice and ingenuity. ' It is as easy,' he adds, ' to call this love of glitter vulgar, as to call his admiration of dukes snobbish ; but the passion is too sincere to deserve any harsh name. . . . There is nothing intrinsically virtuous in preferring a dinner of herbs to the best French cookery.' And Disraeli loved not dinners of herbs.

When he attempts to describe the background in which his characters move, he seems to lack the power of definition. When he sets upon paper the thoughts

and sayings of the personages in his drama, he is as
concise and as finely pointed as any man that ever wrote.
His grasp upon the English sentence tightens.   His
grammar is no longer loose and inaccurate. Whatever mistakes he may commit in narrative and description, he is a master of aphorism.   Open his books
where you will, and you may find a phrase which
deftly sums up his argument, and lingers in your
memory.   'The age of ruins is past.'   'The East
is a career.'   'Youth is a blunder, manhood a struggle,
old age a regret.'   'He who anticipates his century is
generally persecuted when living and is always pilfered
when dead.'   'Beware of endeavouring to be a great
man in a hurry.'   Above all, is he well skilled in
putting a political truth in a few words.   If ever again
the wise among our youth go into politics, they cannot
do better than strengthen their opinions with the
epigrams of Disraeli.   'No Government can long be
secure without a formidable opposition.'   'A sound
Conservative Government.   I understand :   Tory
men and Whig measures.'   'The history of success is
the history of minorities.'   'England is governed by
Downing Street, once it was governed by Alfred and
Elizabeth.'   And many more maxims, at once vivid
and ironic.   Nor is it this gift of aphorism, which
alone set Disraeli upon a high pinnacle.   In movement and character his books may flag ; they never
wholly fail.   Even *The Young Duke*, which it is not easy
to praise, is redressed by the gambling encounter at
Brighton, inspired no doubt by a reading of Casanova.

But, after all, when we think of Disraeli's novels, we think of his famous trilogy, which is secure of remembrance as long as the English tongue is spoken and written.

The trilogy—*Coningsby, Sybil, Tancred*—is in truth an invention in literature. Others have made futile experiments in the political novel. Disraeli alone has achieved it. At the first glance it might seem that the three novels, which make up the trilogy, were too heavily weighted for success. They are romances with a key ; they are stories with a purpose. They might at a first glance seem destined for a brief popularity, and then to be condemned, with other works which excite a quick curiosity, to forgetfulness. *Coningsby* and the rest, having excited and allayed the curiosity, are more ardently read than ever. And they owe their permanence not only to the admirable stories which they tell, but to their political teaching. The purpose, which they acknowledge—to expound the art of government—is perennial, and does not lose its interest, because Disraeli chose as his expositors the men of his own time.

Disraeli, as has been pointed out, was all of a piece. He was the same man, whether he stood upon the hustings or sat down to write in his study. He preached the same gospel in his novels as in the House of Commons, and his historical retrospects, wherever they are set forth, are always worth our praise and our attention. When he took up politics as the business of his life, he had profoundly studied the history of

England.   He had substituted in his mind for the popular empiricism a definite philosophy, based upon the works of Bolingbroke, than whom he could not have found a better guide.   In defiance of all the rules he interpolates in his novels sketches of dead statesmen, which impede the action, if you will, and for their own sake are of the highest worth. Bolingbroke is not the only half-forgotten hero whom he brought back to the light of day.   He did his best also for Shelburne, 'a suppressed character of English history.'   And while he turned his mind willingly to the past, for he recognised the importance of tradition, he did not neglect what was passing about him.   He has left us an imperishable record of contemporary events, in many of which he took an intimate part, and has not allowed what would have been a natural partiality to interfere with justice.   The result is that his trilogy has already acquired the value which belongs to memoirs.   I know not where a better account is to be found of the passing of the Reform Bill than in *Coningsby*.   In the same book Disraeli has painted what none knew so intimately as he, the unfulfilled hopes and aspirations of Young England, the last attempt at political idealism made in this country. And in *Sybil* he castigates the manufacturers of England, who advocated free trade in human lives as well as in corn, who pretended to believe that our national prosperity depended wholly upon the two hours—the difference between ten and twelve—which children under fourteen years of age spent in the mills.

So well did he know the past, so accurately did he understand what was present to him, that he had no difficulty in foretelling the future. ' I observe a party in the State,' said he, ' whose rule is to consent to no change, until it is clamorously called for, and then instantly to yield ; but those are Concessionary, not Conservative principles. This party treats institutions as we do our pheasants, they preserve only to destroy them.' These easy methods of politics were only just beginning when Disraeli wrote *Coningsby*. He foresaw plainly enough a method which has become universal. With an equal prescience he anticipated the weakness of government by Labour. ' You have announced to the millions that their welfare is to be tested by the amount of their wages,' he wrote in *Tancred*. ' Money is to be the cupel of their worth, as it is of all other classes. You propose for their conduct the least ennobling of all impulses. If you have seen an aristocracy invariably become degraded under such influence ; if all the vices of a middle-class may be traced to such an absorbing motive : why are we to believe that the people should be more pure, or that they should escape the catastrophe of the policy which confounds the happiness with the wealth of nations ? ' The passage of the years has but enhanced the truth of this passage. And in further proof that he wrote for our age as well as for his own, we of to-day may utter again in all sincerity the hope, still unrealised, expressed in the last lines of *Sybil*, of a free Monarchy and a privileged and prosperous People.

That such grave words as these should explain and not hinder the romances of Disraeli is the highest tribute to his skill.   And not only did he understand the proper conduct of his fable ; not only did he know how to interweave political philosophy in his fiction ; he possessed a fine talent for the portrayal of character. Leander and the other cooks of Shepherd's Market show a keen perception of their kind, which Thackeray in his Mirobolant panted after and did not reach.   His Tapers and his Tadpoles are eternally enduring types. The characters of the men, whom he had seen and known, are drawn with equal courage and vision. Contrast Rigby and Monmouth with Wenham and Steyne, and you will have no doubt where to award the preference.   Disraeli, in brief, though he pursued the craft of fiction in the leisure snatched from the exacting business of politics, was so lavishly endowed by nature that he claimed and still holds a high and separate place among our novelists.

VII.—A POSTHUMOUS FRAGMENT [1]

The fragment of Disraeli's unfinished novel bears upon every line the true mark of authenticity.   It is alive with wit, and vivid with character.   Brief as it is, it is long enough to give its author the opportunity of realising, by a few deft touches, half a dozen personages, whom we should hardly have known better had the story been carried to its appointed end. Moreover, it is, like all Disraeli's best works, an

[1] An Unpublished Novel (London: *The Times*), 1905.

admirable specimen of satiric presentation.   Its irony
is not savage, as is Fielding's ; perhaps it bites no less
shrewdly because it is expressed with the unfailing
gentleness of good humour.   Here, as elsewhere,
Disraeli turns upon the country, which he governed
and loved, an eye of playful contempt ; with perfect
impartiality he holds up to ridicule an amiable family
of the middle-class, and the noble lord who patronises
it ; and in the background you see faintly outlined
the mysterious denizens of the East, who would
presently have unravelled all the difficulties of the
situation, even if in the process they had brought upon
the world that destruction which, as one of them says,
' must be welcomed in every form.'

In the opening chapter Disraeli once again competes
with Thackeray.   Wilberforce Falconet, like Thomas
Newcome, resides at Clapham, taking an equal pride
in his piety and his pine-apples.   The life of this
respectable merchant in his respectable suburb is
described with exquisite raillery.   His religion does
not dim his sense of a bargain, and, devoted as he is to
psalmody and other exercises, he plays the part at home
of an ' affectionate despot.'   Mrs. Falconet, ' the
founder of many institutions and the soul of all,' is no
unworthy companion for her husband.   ' Schools and
hymns, and Bible-classes and tract distributions and
industrial homes engrossed her life,' and her husband
not only admired her prettiness but sympathised with
her pursuits.   It was no wonder, then, that the young
gentlemen of Clapham Common ' yielded to the

blended spell of religious devotion, female charms, and the most comfortable and piously luxurious domestic establishment in the whole neighbourhood.' And no one of them all was so profoundly religious or so highly accomplished as Joseph Toplady Falconet, the merchant's youngest son.

Now, in Joseph Toplady Falconet, Disraeli has drawn the best portrait of the youthful Gladstone that we have. It is true that it is but a sketch, and that the novelist carries his hero no further than to the door of the House of Commons. *Ex pede Herculem*, and from these few pages we can divine what Gladstone's portrait would have been when Disraeli's hand had perfected it. Moreover, in one sense, Gladstone's career was singularly homogeneous. He changed all his opinions several times ; he never changed his character a jot. Even Lord Morley's excellent *Life* does but repeat with infinite variety the same story. And, since one episode may symbolise a career as clearly as a hundred, the biography of the greatest man must needs suffer from monotony. For me the interest of Lord Morley's *Life of Gladstone* culminates when, in 1832, the hero first stood for Newark. It will be remembered that on that occasion he rode on the mail-coach to London. It was a Sunday, and he beguiled the tedium of the journey by discussing the question of Sunday travelling with a Tory countryman. Not only did he condemn the practice with severity, but he gave some tracts to his companion ; and after this the *Life of Gladstone* is a mere anti-climax. In one moment of confidence he reveals not only what he is, but what he will be.   He announces that he is a law unto himself, that those things are permitted to him which others must avoid as deadly sins.   In the very moment of crime he can present an accomplice with a tract, and in this one action makes clear all the puzzles of an intricate career.

Disraeli knew nothing of the journey to Newark ; he did not spend his years in the study of Gladstone's archives ;   his quick wit discerned the youthful character of the man.   He tells us that Joseph Top-lady Falconet was of singular precocity, 'a grave boy, and scarcely ever known to smile.'   His distinguishing characteristic was ' a complete deficiency in the sense of humour, of which he seemed quite debarred.' Here is a glimpse of the Oxford graduate, who gave away tracts on the London coach.   And the young Falconet resembled his original at many other points. He displayed also a disputatious temper, and was gifted with ' a flow of language, which, even as a child, was ever at command to express his arguments.'   To what could such a youth aspire, after a demure career at public school and university, but to Parliamentary eminence ?   Falconet, too, like Gladstone, was determined to support the Church from without. ' Firm in his faith in an age of dissolving creeds, he wished to believe that he was ordained to vindicate the sublime cause of religious truth.'   He did not long await an opportunity.   A noble lord offered him a seat, he delivered a famous oration on the slave trade in the Red Sea, and his triumph was assured.

Though the portrait is so close to life as to be unmistakable, some ingenious persons have suggested that Joseph Toplady Falconet was intended for Macaulay, because he was born on Clapham Common. The reason is wholly inadequate. It is no part of the novelist's business to cultivate a mechanical accuracy. It is enough for him to tell the essential truth. Though Gladstone went from Liverpool to Eton, he was essentially a native of Clapham. Moreover, Falconet resembles Macaulay in nothing else than a lack of humour, and we do not know why Disraeli should have been at the pains to represent the distinguished historian in the light of a statesman. Nor is Joseph Toplady the only character perfectly realised. The noble lord is suggested in a few strokes —urbane, witty, and not a little contemptuous. ' I wish I had asked permission to bring Lady Bertram with me,' says he, after the family party, at which a long grace before and after meat had taken the place of a religious ceremony. And you feel that Disraeli is smiling at his lordship, as well as at his zealous hosts. Still better is Lord Gaston, a clever reminiscence of the early 'forties, a clever, disillusioned young man, who might have played his part in *Coningsby* or *Sybil*. He is tired of politics, because he is convinced that ' Parliaments are played out.' And the failure of Parliaments is not the worst sign of a feeble age. ' Nothing is so exhausted,' says he, ' as the human race

itself,' and the exhaustion is not an affair of yesterday.
' The fact is,' he has discovered, ' that man has really
never very much taken to this globe.' The one
solution of the inextricable tangle of things is found
by Mr. Hartmann, a German banker, and his friend
the Unknown. When they are on the stage, Disraeli
drops his irony, and writes with a seriousness which
Sidonia was wont to inspire. Their remedy for all
evils is destruction. Not for nothing did they
come out of Jewry. They detect ' indications of
habitual dearth in this globe which are encouraging.'
It is their hope to achieve the total extinction of the
human race. The mysterious Unknown, of whom
we catch but a glimpse, would doubtless have expressed
more fully Disraeli's own half-despondent, half-
humorous cynicism. ' If anything is to be really done
in this world,' says he, ' it must be done by visionaries ;
men who see the future, and make the future because
they see it. What I really feared about—was that
he had the weakness of believing in politics.' Briefly,
there is no character that does not at once excite
and baffle our curiosity. Lady Bertram and Lady
Ermyntrude, the destined bride, perhaps, of Joseph,
would have grown into living people under their
author's hands, and Mr. Chatterley promised to be
a rival of Taper and Tadpole.

Disraeli was ever champion of the young, and it was
his greatest happiness to preserve the youth of his
intellect unimpaired until the end. This fragment,
the last that he wrote, is as young as epigram and satire

can make it. If never a scrupulous writer, always, as I have said, a master of phrase, he proved that the gift, which he displayed so brilliantly in his trilogy, was still his own. When Toplady is eager to return once more to the discussion of the slave trade, 'I think I would leave the Red Sea alone,' said the Earl. 'It was a miracle that saved us from being drowned in it before.' And how just is this comment upon the young statesman ! 'With all his abilities and acquirements, Joseph Toplady Falconet was essentially a prig, and among prigs there is a freemasonry which never fails. All the prigs spoke of him as the coming man.' Again, when the Unknown is pleading the cause of annihilation, Mr. Hartmann suggests that among the Chinese about the port of London there must be the elements of a congregation. 'The English like a congregation,' says he. 'The moment there is a congregation, they think the affair practical.' So to whatever page you turn in this unfinished novel, you find flashes of the old Disraeli, and regret only that what might have been a masterpiece of political fiction is but a brilliant fragment.

OUTLINES

JAMES HARRINGTON

WHEN James Harrington sat himself down to compose *Oceana*, he was not, like Plato and Sir Thomas More, held captive by his imagination. He cherished no hope of amusing or solacing his readers. Though he followed his great predecessors in giving a romantic shape and a romantic name to his commonwealth, his aim was not artistic, but sternly practical. He was no poet that he should embroider his thoughts with the flowers of fancy. Not even the title, *Oceana*, could deceive the unwary. His object was to sketch the England of his own day, dominated as it was by Oliver Cromwell, and craving, as he believed, for safeguards against the tyranny of one man. He was urgent that the remedies proposed should be applied without delay, and he had so profound a faith in them that for their sake he was willing to wear chains and to be deprived of the air of heaven.

If Plato and More dreamed dreams and saw visions, Harrington was content to draw up a State paper. He was an inductive philosopher, who had no doubt that by writing and thinking and suggesting you could really make this stubborn world happier and better. With a great patience he collected such materials as seemed to him necessary for a judgment. He made the grand tour with the avowed object of seeing how other countries were governed. ' No man,' he said with some truth, ' can be a politician, except he be first a historian or a traveller.' Harrington was both. Not only had he seen men and cities ; he had read books. From the Classics he had learned the doctrine of republicanism, which he guarded jealously unto the end. Even above the Classics he placed Macchiavelli, ' the only politician of later ages.' He was no more easily to be turned aside from his enterprise by senti- ment than Macchiavelli himself. On no other founda- tion would he build a constitution than the foundation of facts. ' He that will erect a Commonwealth,' said he, ' against the judgment of Macchiavelli is obliged to give such reasons for his enterprise as must not go a-begging.' His enterprise was in no danger. He bowed the knee in all humility and with a constant heart to the author of *The Prince*.

Harrington was not an artist. His work will never be read for the pleasure it might impart. It is an exposition of solid doctrine with a misleading name, and no more. If it be esteemed, it must be esteemed as a guide to good government, as a handbook for such sanguine mortals as believe that they can do good to the State by the mere utterance of formulæ. The ingenuity displayed in the performance of Harrington's hopeless task is evident, though nobody will agree with the author's own estimate of its scientific finality. He did not scruple to compare himself with the ' famous Hervey.' The blood circulated in the human frame before Hervey discovered it. The truth, which he expounded, was as old as the race. And Harrington, also, claimed to be a scientific observer, who had made clear for ever the inevitable laws which govern society.

The first of the dogmas, which he preached with a tireless resolution, was that, 'as is the proportion or balance of dominion or property in land, such is the nature of the Empire.' This harmony or balance he believed to be essential to the welfare of the State. If it did not exist, it must be assured either by a change of government or by a wider distribution of property.[1] Before all things Harrington had faith in the landed gentry. 'There is something first,' he wrote, 'in the making of the Commonwealth, there is the governing of it, and last of all is the leading of its armies ; which (though there be great divines, great lawyers, great men in all professions) seems to be peculiar only to the genius of a gentleman.' The

[1] Pepys attended a meeting of Harrington's club on 17th January 1659-60. 'So I went to the Coffee Club,' says he, 'and heard very good discourse ; it was in answer to Mr. Harrington's answer, who said that the state of the Roman Government was not a settled government, and so it was no wonder that the balance of property was in one hand, and the command in another, it being therefore always in a posture of war ; but it was carried by ballot, that it was a steady government, though it is true by the voices it had been carried before that it was an unsteady government ; so to-morrow it is to be proved by the opposition that the balance lay in one hand, and the government in another.' A wise comment, which is true of all the debating societies that ever there were.

contempt with which our modern democracy receives
such statements as this does not in the least affect their
truth. For the rest, he believed, with many other
honest pedants, that the ballot was a cure for most
political evils, that there should be a proper rotation of
officers, since ' the prolongation of magistracy is the
ruin of popular government,' that elections should
always be conducted indirectly through electoral
bodies, and that the functions of the two chambers
which he proposed should be rigidly separated. The
Senate, or Upper Chamber, as he devised it, had for
its function to propose and discuss measures, upon
which the Lower House was invited to vote in silence.
It is an artifice which does not meet with the approval
of our modern demagogues, and which when Sieyès
introduced it into the French Constitution aroused
the fierce contempt of Napoleon. ' Three hundred
men who never speak,' said he. ' What an absurdity ! '
It seems less an absurdity than a counsel of perfection,
and whatever experiment may be tried in the future,
it assuredly will not be Harrington's of a speechless
House of Commons. Unless only the dumb were
eligible for election the assembly could not exist for
a day without breaking the law of silence.

There is a deep tragedy in the persistence of those
who think they can make men and countries happier
by paper devices. If we lived in a vacuum, secure
from the popular breeze, if our leaders were cut and
clipped to an invariable standard, there might be some
profit in such speculations as Harrington's. In the

world that we know they are made ridiculous in a moment by the breath of accident or the sudden appearance of a hero.   Cromwell, at any rate, being a man of action, knew how to deal with Harrington.   At first *Oceana* was confiscated in the press.   Then, when it was printed, by the intercession of Lady Claypole, Cromwell's daughter, who 'acted the part of a princess very naturally,' Cromwell properly made light of it.   'The gentleman had like to repair him out of his power,' he said, 'but what he got by the sword he would not quit for a little paper shot.' Harrington, on the other hand, was not disheartened. After Cromwell's death he did his best to turn his written constitution into a reality, and cheerfully went to prison, when Charles II. returned to power, for the principles which he believed to be founded in truth itself.

It is Aubrey who gives us the best account of Harrington, as of many others, and the wisest of all gossips makes it clear that Harrington's obliging manners and pleasant disposition carried him further in the general esteem than his political speculations. Republican though he was, he remained the devoted subject of Charles I. even unto the scaffold.   He was the friend of men so far apart in thought and policy as Marvell and L'Estrange.   At the Rota Club, where he instructed his friends in the use of 'the balloting-box,' he won the respect which comes of a prudent moderation.   Aubrey tells us that Harrington 'had every night a meeting at the (then)

Turke's Head, in the New Pallace-yard, where they
take water, the next house to the staires, at one
Miles's, where was purposely made a large ovall-
table, with a passage in the middle for Miles to
deliver his Coffee. About it sate his disciples and
the virtuosi. The discourses in this kind were the
most ingeniose, and smart that ever I heard, or
expect to heare, and bandied with great eagernesse :
the arguments in the Parliament-house were but
flatt to it. Here we had (very formally) a balloting-
box, and balloted how things should be carried by
way of tentamens. The room was every evening
full as it could be cramm'd.' Upon General Monk's
coming in, the Club vanished with many other
chimerical schemes. For the rest, Harrington's
mild disposition was universally confessed. Even in
the madness which followed his imprisonment he
displayed no worse 'phansy than his perspiration
turned to flies, and sometimes to bees—*ad cetera
sobrius.*' So, living 'in the Little Ambrey (a faire
house on the left hand), which looks into the Deane's
yard,' he entertained his friends, 'in his conversations
very friendly, and facetious, and hospitable.' Once
an influence in America and France, he runs a risk
of being forgotten to-day, and he will be fortunate,
if he still keeps a place, a dreamer of dreams, in the
archæology of politics.

THE TRIMMER

POLITICS is the profession of the second-rate. The man of genius strays into it by accident. We do not need the fingers of both hands to count the statesmen who have served England since the seventeenth century. The Ministers who have served themselves are like the sands for number. And from this mob of mediocrities it is not strange that very few writers have emerged. It is not an extravagant claim that they should have some mastery of literary expression. Words are the material of their craft. They know not how to use them save in the cause of rhetoric. Charles James Fox, the world was told, was an accomplished man of letters. To hear him discourse of the Classics was almost as fine an experience as to see him take the bank at faro. And then he wrote a book, and his fame was blown away like a bubble. Halifax and Bolingbroke, Burke and Disraeli — these are secure of remembrance. Where shall you find a fifth ?

The writings of Halifax are valuable, then, because they are packed into the double experience of author and statesman. His work and his life are bound up in the closest intimacy. His style was the reflection of his own sturdy mind. Montaigne's *Essays*, he

tells us, is ' the book in the world he is best entertained
with,' and what he writes of that author is exactly
true of himself. ' He let his mind have its full flight,'
says he of Montaigne, 'and sheweth by a generous
kind of negligence that he did not write for praise,
but to give the world a true picture of himself and of
mankind.' Montaigne's ambition was the ambition
of Halifax, and if the flight of the Trimmer's mind
was not as lofty as the flight of Montaigne's, it is
because he kept by preference closer to the ground of
reality.

Thus his manner of writing differs not from the
manner of Montaigne. The author of the *Essays*
boasts somewhere that his style is *soldatesque*. *Soldatesque* also is the style of Halifax. He, too, wrote like
a man of action. He was, happily, incapable of that
chief vice of politics and of letters—rhetoric. He had
not a quick ear for the music of prose, and doubtless
he spent little time in regretting his lack of harmony.
But he understood the art of cramming a brief sentence
with meaning as few writers have understood it. The
concision of his phrase is his distinction ; it is never
mean or wire-drawn. Though he wastes no words, he
spares no sense, and makes the English tongue a ready
servant of his wisdom. There is a weight in his writings which has nothing to do with the weight of their
thought, which is weighty enough. He proves on
every page the directness of one in authority. His style
possesses something of the quality which you will find
in Napoleon's letters or Wellington's despatches. He

does not disdain the plain phrases of practical life—
phrases that he would have used in common talk.
'The Popish humour,' he says, 'was too tough to
be totally expell'd.' Or of the Treaty of Aix-la-
Chapelle : ''twas a forc'd put.' And as if to make
always this active impression upon our minds, he
delights in the use of grave spondees and heavy mono-
syllables. His sentences never trip ; they march, and
march most often to the victory of convincing his
readers.

Men called him a Trimmer, and in a sense the
name was justified. Halifax was sure that he could
serve the State, whatever party was in power. He
believed, like Wellington, that he was necessary to
carry on the King's Government. At any rate, he
turned the vice of trimming into a virtue with much
spirit and a mordant irony. He gave the word a
weight and purpose of his own. 'This innocent
word Trimmer,' he writes, 'signifieth no more than
this : That if men are together in a Boat, and one
part of the Company would weigh it down on one
side, another would make it lean as much to the
contrary ; it happeneth there is a third Opinion, of
those who conceive it would do as well, if the Boat
went even, without endangering the Passengers ; now
'tis hard to imagine by what Figure of Language or
by what Rule in Sense this cometh to be a fault, and
it is much more a wonder it should be thought a
Heresy.'

Such was his view of a Trimmer, and his tract, *The*

Trimmer's Opinion of the Laws and Government,
is worthy to stand upon the shelf with Macchiavelli's
Prince.   As a treatise of State, it neither distresses us
by moderation nor perplexes us with ingenuity.   The
Trimmer is the whole-hearted champion of the
Crown and of what was once ' our blessed Constitution.'   He sees in its ' happy mixture ' our felicity
and the envy of our neighbour.   ' The Crown hath
power sufficient to protect our Liberties,' he thinks.
' The people have so much Liberty as is necessary to
make them useful to the Crown.'   Alas !   We have
lost our felicity ;   our neighbour has no longer a just
cause of envy.   ' Our blessed Constitution,' as the
Trimmer knew and praised it, has been broken in
pieces, and seems to have but a slender chance of being
put together again.

   ' The politics of this country,' says one of Halifax's
editors, ' have altered very little, one would say, since
the days of the Exclusion Bill.'   It is difficult to agree
with him.   The works of Halifax have no meaning
for the demagogues of to-day.   His *Political Thoughts
and Reflections* are addressed to a race of men rapidly
becoming extinct.   A writer who objected to party,
because ' it turneth all thought into talking instead
of doing,' and who declared that ' the angry buzz of
a multitude is one of the bloodiest noises in the world,'
is clearly unintelligible to our hardy Radicals.   Moreover, Halifax was a patriot.   For him politics meant
the service of his master and his country.   He was
incapable of putting up his Constitution to auction on

the public hustings, and knocking it down to the highest bidder. His discourse is never of votes. He preferred ' the smell in our native earth ' before all the perfumes of the East. When he sang the praise of England he struck a lyrical note rarely heard in his works. ' Our Trimmer,' said he, ' is far from idolatry in other things, in one thing only he cometh near it, his Country is in some degree his Idol ; he doth not worship the Sun, because 'tis not peculiar to us, it rambles round the world, and is less kind to us than others ; but for the Earth of England, tho perhaps inferior to that of many places abroad, to him there is a Divinity in it, and he would rather dye than see a spire of English Grass trampled down by a Foreign Trespasser.' These words are gibberish to those who believe that military service is a disgrace, and who find a profit in friendship with their country's enemies.

And none knew better than Halifax that the safety of England depended upon her supremacy on the ocean. His *Rough Draught of a New Model at Sea*, written in 1694, will still serve as a piece of gospel for our Navy. He insists that ' as the importance of being strong at Sea was ever very great, so in our present Circumstances it is grown to be much greater ; because, as formerly our Force of Shipping contributed greatly to our Trade and Safety, so now it is become necessary to our very Being.' These words have lost none of their truth in the years that have passed since they were written, and his exhortation should be remembered by all those who have the welfare of England at heart. ' It may be said now to England '—thus he wrote—' Martha, Martha, thou art busy about many things, but one thing is necessary. To the Question, What shall we do to be saved in this World ? there is no other Answer but this, Look to your Moate.' Such was the same council of Halifax, and if we neglect it, then surely are we lost.

Thus it is that the works of Halifax are moss-grown with a sad antiquity. Neither time nor the apostasy of our age can impair his close-packed eloquence and his civic wisdom. An honesty of mind distinguished him, whether he gave advice to his daughter or sketched the character of his sauntering King, as finely balanced a portrait of a King as has ever been made, or proved himself a truer, greater master of the maxim than La Rochefoucauld himself. And all who care for English letters and the history of English politics may look back with pride to Halifax, the grand-father of that Toryism whereof Bolingbroke was father, and Disraeli the distinguished son.

GEORGE JEFFREYS

GEORGE JEFFREYS, afterwards Baron Jeffreys of Wem and Keeper of the Great Seal, was born near Wrexham in Denbighshire, a year before Charles the First's head fell upon the block. Of honourable parentage, he received the best education that the times afforded, and being a boy of quick parts and tireless energy, he made the most of his opportunities. An injudicious historian, intent upon prejudice, has discovered that 'at marbles and leap-frog he was known to take undue advantages.' Such fables as this may be speedily dismissed, and it is enough to say that three great schools claim him as their pupil—Shrewsbury, St. Paul's, and Westminster. at which last he came under the rod of the admirable Busby ; that after a year spent at Trinity College, Cambridge, where doubtless he recognised that academic distinction was not for him, he went to seek his fortune in London ; and that, admitted to the Inner Temple, 19th May 1663, he never looked back until he had become, in the phrase of his best biographer, 'the top fiddler of the town.'

The London to which he came could not but have excited the ambition of so brisk and lively a youth. Splendour and gaiety had come back with the restored

Monarch. Mistress Stewart had but yesterday replaced my Lady Castlemaine in the King's affection. The Duke of Monmouth stood so high in favour that he openly boasted of his succession and set the mode of pleasure and magnificence. ' God knows what will be the end of it,' said Pepys, whose doubt was presently resolved upon the field of Sedgemoor. Meanwhile the playhouses had once more opened their doors to present the masterpieces of Shakespeare and Jonson and to hail the rising genius of John Dryden. Not only was there in the brilliant life of the time the best incentive to enterprise, there was also a career open to all the talents ; and no man need despair of the future if he had but a ready courage and a determination to serve his King.

Now, George Jeffreys was born at the very moment appropriate to his temper. He was handsome, adroit, and unscrupulous. Above all, he was gifted with the genius of prosperity, and he measured his age with perfect accuracy. His sense of humour, moreover, was so sharp that he could laugh at penury ; and if, as North tells us, his beginnings were low, we may be sure that from his garret window in the Temple he looked confidently towards Whitehall. He could make himself at home in all companies, he would drink with anybody who would crack a bottle—even with the shy attorneys that haunted the taverns of Fleet Street,—and he was a churl indeed who did not surrender to the charm of his voice and the sparkle of his wit. Called to the bar in 1668, he practised at the Old Bailey and the Sessions, where he cultivated that talent for impudent browbeating and scurrile ribaldry, wherein he surpassed the most turbulent of his contemporaries, even the eminent Scroggs himself. At first, if we may believe North, the briefs came haltingly. Jeffreys, unabashed, ' used to sit in coffee-houses and order his man to come and tell him that company attended him at his chambers ; at which he would huff and say : Let them stay a little ; I will come presently.' This made a show of business. The show was soon turned to reality, and not even his love of sedition hindered his advance.

Though we must accept the legends of biography with the utmost caution, there is little doubt that Jeffreys, like many other heroes of active and original intelligence, began his career as a sturdy champion of the people. The love of kings, which was presently to make and unmake his fortune, was not yet aflame in his breast. He would drink on his knees any toast ' to the good old cause ' or ' the immortal memory of Old Noll.' This disloyalty may have been a mere indiscretion of youth, or was assumed, perchance, to catch clients. Whatever its origin, it was laid aside as soon as Jeffreys's affability had won him the patron-age of the great. A man of the world while yet a boy, a diner-out welcome at all tables, he soon found his way to the Court. Will Chiffinch, ' the trusty page of the back stairs,' whispered his name to the King ; the Duchess of Portsmouth smiled approval upon him ;

and at twenty-three he was Common-Sergeant of
the City of London.   In quick succession he was
appointed Solicitor to the Duke of York, Recorder
of London, and Chief Justice of Chester.   He
discharged his duties with courage and energy,
caring not for the countenance of any man.   'This
is a bold fellow,' said King Charles, with perfect
truth ; and he was bold to some purpose when the
Popish Plot and the misfortunes in which it involved the country gave him the great opportunity
of his life.

It is a whimsical paradox that the age of Charles II.,
devoted as it was to the pursuit of gaiety and pleasure,
was yet darkened by a religious fanaticism which
even the good sense and easy tolerance of the King
failed to mitigate.   On the one side were thousands
of citizens who, still remembering the freedom
of the Commonwealth, acknowledged the informal
leadership of convinced republicans, such as Algernon
Sidney, and who were ready to die rather than
bend the knee to the Pope.   On the other was a
King who, while professing obedience to the English
Church, cherished a secret sympathy with Rome, and
an heir presumptive to the throne whose papistry was
unconcealed.   The Protestants, no doubt, had the
juster cause, but in policy and honour neither side
may claim a superiority, and the machinations of that
perjured rascal Titus Oates sufficed to arouse an
unreasoning fury against the Catholics.   Oates himself was feasted, pensioned, and proclaimed 'the

Saviour of the Nation.' No attempt was made at the outset to check his falsehoods or to sift his evidence. He had but to open his mouth, and he was believed infallible. Even Jeffreys himself, loyal Abhorrer though he was, was 'surprised' into acquiescence, though his shrewd knowledge of men soon corrected a false impression. The worst consequence of Oates's success was that the other side made instant reprisals, and for some years the courts of law were given over to the examination of rebels and dissenters.

This was Jeffreys's chance. There was nothing in the world he hated so bitterly as he hated the dissenters. He had a nose for them, he boasted : he could smell a Presbyterian at forty miles ; and he attacked them, first as prosecutor, then as judge, with all the energy and resource of a violent temper. The brutality wherewith he assailed his enemies was unexampled, even in his own age, because, though his contemporaries would gladly have followed in his steps, not one could scale the lofty height of his insolence. He jested, he bullied, he denounced— always in 'the sweet and powerful voice' which, as Lord Campbell allows, claimed attention, irrespective of what he said. His tongue and brain were never idle. He conspicuously proved his talent in the trial of Colledge, the London joiner, whom he covered with ridicule, disconcerted with quips, and at last saw triumphantly convicted. Three years later (1683) he assisted in the prosecution of the miscreant Lord

William Russell,[1] and in reward for his zeal was appointed Lord Chief Justice of England.

It is for his conduct of this high office that Jeffreys has been most fiercely condemned, and if he be judged by the standard of to-day, little can be said in his defence. Though as prosecuting counsel he eagerly sought convictions, he sought them with infinitely greater passion as judge. Already proficient in the art of cross-examination, he practised it from the bench with a skill and ferocity which, in the opinion of experts, entitle him to the glory of having perfected that not too amiable method of justice. Worse still, he took for granted the guilt of every prisoner brought before him, and, contemptuous in his certitude, he did not scruple to relieve his sombre duty with flashes of rough humour and coarse repartee, for which perhaps a court of justice is not the best place. Ugly as his violence against a prisoner on trial for his life appears to our humaner minds, we must attempt to view Jeffreys in his own environment, and we shall

---

[1] The Hon. Vicary Gibbs in his *Complete Peerage* sets Lord William Russell in his proper place. ‘It is calculated to lessen sympathy,’ he writes, ‘with this “ornament of his age,” and idol of the Whigs, when it is remembered that he violently opposed the King’s remitting, and affected to doubt his power to remit, that portion of the penalty for high treason, which involved disembowelling alive in the case of the aged Lord Strafford, whose crime was being a Roman Catholic. Charles II. showed more mercy, when “the wheel came full circle,” than this since canonised ruffian had been willing to extend to the victim of a pretended plot, which he and his political friends, with the aid of Titus Oates, exploited in their party’s interest.’

then have no difficulty in modifying our judgment. In the first place, he was called to the bench less to administer justice than to do the King's business. In the second place, 'a criminal trial in those days,' as Sir James Stephen, the most eminent authority, has pointed out, 'was not unlike a race between the King and the prisoner, in which the King had a long start, and the prisoner was heavily weighted.' In brief, Jeffreys did but adhere to the practice of his age ; and he has been held up to obloquy ever since because, being incomparably better endowed in wits and style than his fellows, he has filled a larger space in history and legend than they could ever hope to fill.

Sidney and Armstrong were justly punished. In the trials of Rosewell and Richard Baxter, Jeffreys allowed his hatred of dissenters to outstrip the bounds of judgment and decency. Rosewell, a gentleman and a scholar, made an admirably moderate defence, but no sobriety could check the flaunts and gibes of the judge, who was bent upon a conviction and got it. Happily, Sir John Talbot, Rosewell's friend, had the ear of the King. 'Sir,' said he to Charles, 'if your Majesty suffers this man to die, we are none of us safe in our houses' ; and Charles, declaring that the prisoner must live, bade Jeffreys find some way to bring him off. Confronted by Baxter, Jeffreys was yet more ferocious, attempting to atone for the weakness of the evidence by the strength of his invective. 'Yonder stands Oates in the pillory,' he exclaimed, 'and says he suffers for the truth ; and so says Baxter ;

but if Baxter did but stand on the other side of the pillory with him, I would say two of the greatest rogues and rascals in the kingdom stood there.' A reference to Baxter's sympathy with bishops delighted the Lord Chief Justice. ' Baxter for bishops ! ' said he ; ' that 's a merry conceit indeed ! Turn to it, turn to it.' And when Baxter would fain have addressed the court, Jeffreys broke out in his best manner : ' Richard ! Richard ! dost thou think we 'll hear thee poison the court ? Richard, thou art an old fellow, an old knave ; thou hast written books enough to load a cart. Hadst thou been whipt out of thy writing trade forty years ago, it had been happy.' After these eloquent tirades, Baxter was found guilty by the jury, was absolved even of the light sentence which Jeffreys imposed, and thus by a piece of good fortune, which he did not deserve, the judge was saved from the consequences of two infamous actions.

Meanwhile James ii. had succeeded to the throne, and Jeffreys, now raised to the peerage, served a fiercer, more implacable master. With a heart as hard as marble, and a brain as narrow as the edge of a sword-blade, James was nevertheless a man of force, and a sincere, if misguided, patriot. He would have been an excellent King of Spain, where he might have divided his allegiance between his country and the Pope ; he was completely unfitted by character and sympathy to govern England, which would on no account tolerate an understanding with Rome.

Moreover, in the attainment of his ends he knew neither policy nor compromise. He was so harsh a fanatic that he would have rejected pity even had he deemed it profitable, and he found in Jeffreys the willing instrument of his severity. Nor was the opportunity, which both master and man desired, long in coming. On 11th June 1685, Monmouth landed at Lyme-Regis ; nine days later he took the title of King, in defiance of his principles ; on 6th July his army of peasants was defeated at Sedgemoor ; and early in September, Lord Jeffreys set out to do his thorough-stitch work in the west.

Now, one of Jeffreys's most striking qualities was a sense of drama. He moved naturally with pomp and circumstance, and when he went down into the rebellious counties he omitted nothing that might add to the horror of his apparition. He was invested with military as well as with judicial powers, and throughout the ' campaign,' as James called it, he comported himself rather as a soldier than as a judge. The agony of a painful disease embittered his speech, and the harangues wherewith he opened his courts of justice exceeded all his previous efforts in rage, scurrility, and contempt.

A supporter of Monmouth, to whom unhappily we owe the sole account of Jeffreys's campaign, has not scrupled to represent it as an orgy of blood and brandy. This is obviously the language of passionate exaggeration. The number of rebels condemned by Jeffreys was two hundred and fifty-one—less by fifty than the King's soldiers who fell at Sedgemoor. Nor can the Whigs pretend that the victims of the judge's anger were innocent of rebellion ; rather they proclaim them noble because they rose in open revolt against their King. Now, to offer armed violence to the State, even for a just cause, was a crime in the seventeenth century, as it is in the twentieth, and there was no adherent of Monmouth but deserved the death he suffered. For the rebellion was no holiday parade. Not merely was Monmouth proclaimed King, but James was denounced as an enemy, a traitor, and a fratricide. The most clement monarch that ever graced a throne could hardly regard this denunciation with equanimity ; and James, knowing no clemency at all, rightly sent Jeffreys into the west on his mission of blood. We may deplore the King's imprudence ; we cannot find language too severe wherein to condemn the greed and venality which sold pardons for vast sums of money ; to call the Chief Justice's executions in the west judicial murders, as historians are wont to call them, is to be guilty of a vain, dishonest prejudice.

So Jeffreys, having done his work without stint or pity, came back from the west to claim his reward, conscious that he had both served his master loyally, and meted out justice with a fair, if heavy, hand. And when misfortune overtook the King and his judge, each attempted to shift the blame of an unpopular policy upon the other. In each complaint there is a suspicion of truth. The severity, no doubt, was dictated by the King. The faults of style and taste were all Jeffreys's own. However the responsibility be divided, a speedy retribution overtook them both. Though Jeffreys was given the Great Seal, and for three years carried out his master's policy with disastrous industry, on 11th December 1688, James deserted his capital, and the Chancellor fled before the fury of the mob. The last act of Jeffreys's life was as dramatic as the Bloody Assize itself. Not even in ruin did his sense of theatrical effect desert him. Disguised as a sailor, he took refuge on a coal-barge ; then, wearied of confinement after a single night, he made his appearance at the Red Cow, in Anchor and Hope Alley, and ordered a pot of ale. There he was recognised by a scrivener whom he had once browbeat in court, and who promised then that he would never forget ' the terrors of that man's face.' Betrayed by the scrivener, he was brought before the Lord Mayor, and at the Mansion House he played his last trick of nonchalance. He so profoundly impressed the Mayor that he was bidden to dinner, and danced with his daughter, even while the people clamoured without. Flight was imperative, and Jeffreys was hustled into the Tower, the one corner of safety left him, where he cheated vengeance by a sudden and untimely death.

He was, as I have said, of rare talent and fascination. Though his legal abilities have been eclipsed by the scandal of his career, his bitterest enemies confess him a man of excellent parts, a lawyer of vigorous understanding and impressive eloquence. His judgments in civil cases were remarkable for their shrewdness and sanity, and though when he accepted the Great Seal he knew little of Chancery business, his native wit carried him triumphant through all his difficulties. The rough side of his tongue he reserved sternly for his profession, and the ease of his manners, conspicuous even in a courtly age, made him apt for all societies. That he was of a harsh temper may be admitted ; it is true that he was determined to succeed by the most convenient avenue ; but history affords no evidence that he was an unjust judge, delighting in the shedding of innocent blood.   His heaviest misfortunes were to serve a cruel, honest, impolitic prince, to touch the imagination of an ignorant populace, and to find a sentimental biographer in a miscreant whom he had condemned to be whipped at the cart's tail in every market-town of Dorsetshire.   However, a man is always nearer to truth than a monster, and the Jeffreys of fact wins our faith and holds our interest more easily than the zealot of blasphemy and murder imagined by Mr. Tutchin, Lord Macaulay, and other eminent historians.

AN ELDERLY TORY

FEW men of letters have been more wantonly misunderstood than Voltaire. He has been denounced as an atheist, and praised publicly by the National Assembly as the scourge of atheists and fanatics. To these he has appeared a devil of mockery, to those the loyal defender of the rights of man. By one writer, an Englishman with a genius for confusion, he has been described as not a man but a movement! In vain shall we search the pages of biography for an unhappier definition. Though literature was in his blood, Voltaire was above all things a man, a man whose passionate sense of life was quick unto the end, whose keen perception of life's drama was never dimmed. With a frank self-consciousness he cast himself for the chief part, now in the farce, now in the comedy of a multi-coloured career, and played it admirably. Not even when he faced the footlights in his great scene with Frederick the Great was he asked to surrender the pride of place.

As a writer, he has been the victim of his own garrulity. Rabelais and Montaigne, far greater than he in thought and style, claim the added good fortune of being the masters of one book apiece. There is

R

nothing of theirs that we are asked to discard. We may read them from beginning to end in the same mood of understanding and without the fatigue of criticism. It is not our business to separate the wheat from the chaff, where all is good golden grain. Between Voltaire and his readers there stand, grave and menacing, his sixty (or is it his eighty ?) volumes. We are forced to distinguish and define, to condemn this and accept that, within the narrow canon of approval. We may take it that the great mass of Voltaire's writings is dead beyond the hope of resurrection. It is not likely that a human eye will ever again be thrown upon his poor philosophies or his turgid epics. He who himself was the finest of comedians had not the gift of making comedies. His infamous libel upon Jeanne d'Arc suggests that there are some subjects which satire cannot touch. But when we have thrown his philosophies and his epics, his libel and his comedies, aside, how much remains to awake our enthusiasm !

Of no writer can it be said with greater truth that the half is greater than the whole. His histories may still be studied as models of balanced and lucid narrative. His letters hold an honoured place even among the greatest. Above all, his fame rests securely upon his two stories, *Zadig* and *Candide*, those little masterpieces of swift irony and crystal-clear criticism which, in a hundred and fifty years, have lost not one spark of their brilliance, and which will perish only with the death of the French tongue. If we might give to Voltaire and Diderot two books apiece, and exclude the erudition which was their pride, they would stand unchallenged in their century. *Candide* and *Zadig* are still supreme, and what but they are worthy to be set on the same shelf with the *Neveu de Rameau* and the *Paradoxe* ?

There is another reason why the men of letters of a later age have dared to belittle Voltaire. He inflicted upon the French language the same injury which Cicero inflicted upon Latin : he reduced it to a standard. He made easy the path of literary ambition. He put a perfect instrument into the hands of many who could not think and who had nothing to say. Thus out of perfection came commonness, and Voltaire has incurred some of the blame which should attach to his apes. And at last the finished ease of Voltaire is falling effectively under the ban of censure. The prose-writers of France are discovering that there are other models than the author of *Candide*, and in the supremacy of Montaigne and Bossuet and St. Simon we may forget even a momentary resentment which the polished surface of Voltaire's style has inspired.

I have said that Voltaire was a comedian, and never did he play the comedy of life with a better zest than when he gave himself the rôle of the Hermit of Ferney. It was a rôle whose irony rejoiced his heart. Tired of kings and great men, tired also of the people and its strife, he sought the solace of a country life, like the wise and elderly Tory that he was. At Ferney

he found all that was grateful to his soul. What a
prospect it was for an apostle of ' free thought,' a
champion of the rights of man, to inhabit a castle,
beetling with crenelles, turrets, and machicoulis !
There he could play the seigneur with what magnificence he would, and indulge the thought of hanging
from his lofty walls the priests of Baal, who would
gladly, if they could, have led him to the stake.   From
the very first he interpreted his duties and privileges, as
seigneur de paroisse, in a liberal spirit.   He was determined to be the real father of his people.   If he were
at last a despot, the thing of all others which he once
hated, he would show that despotism and benevolence
are not incompatible.

He gladly took up the burden of his state.   He
drained the marshes which environed his castle.
Believing with Colbert that agriculture alone was
not a sufficient basis of sound finance, he established
factories of silk stockings in his village, and presently
encouraged the making of clocks and watches.
Under his auspices, Ferney became a prosperous
and God-fearing village.   In the true spirit of an
English squire, he took the Church under his own
protection.   He attended his Church, in solemn
state, every Sunday, dressed out in such a garb,
he told the Prince de Ligne, as gave him an air
of nobility !   His patronage, perhaps, was misunderstood by the clergy.   He thought that he had loaded
the curé with benefits when he had bidden him
drink a glass of wine in the kitchen.   The curé

drank his wine, and resented the philosopher's interference with his pastoral duties. Once upon a time, when drunken villagers had robbed Voltaire of his firewood, the philosopher preached a sermon in the Church, after receiving absolution, upon the heinous sins of drunkenness and thieving, and was surprised, no doubt, when the curé of Ferney joined with the philosophers of Paris in condemning his conduct. Alas ! these good folk understood not irony.

And at Ferney, Voltaire was a veritable patriarch ; he delighted to pose before his visitors as a son of the soil. ' I am only a peasant,' said he to those who came to Paris to see him enact his new part, the man who once upon a time was angry with Congreve for saying, ' I am only a gentleman.' With a gesture of pride he would point to his woods, his vines, and his plantations. He would discourse eloquently to the friends of other days concerning his farm and his *basse-cour*. He would offer them, superbly smiling, fresh milk to drink, and declare that he placed himself far higher in the rank of patriarchs than Abraham or Jacob. It is small wonder, then, that his immense prestige and his enviable seigneury drew upon Voltaire the eyes of Europe. To the young English aristocrat, especially, he was long the object of pious pilgrimages. There were few grand tours in which Ferney did not find a place, and Voltaire's table-talk is solemnly recorded in many a dull book of travels. Thus he lived on to a lean old age, happy in the honour paid him by rich and poor, enlivened by the law-suits which he cultivated with the keenness of an amateur, and by his quarrels with the clergy, which kept the point of his wit and irony still sharp. Nor at his death was the work of his old age undone. Ferney did not lose all the importance he had given it, and when at the Congress of Vienna a new frontier was drawn, it was due to the sole glory of Voltaire that the district of Gex was not taken from France. To few philosophers or poets has so high a compliment been paid. In a like spirit of sacrifice to the Muses the house of Pindarus was spared, 'when temple and tower went to the ground.'

JEAN-JACQUES ROUSSEAU

IT was by a strange paradox that some years since the French Government publicly honoured the memory of Jean-Jacques Rousseau, the man who most bitterly despised civic order and the decent traditions of human life. By unveiling a monument in the Panthéon, it bore testimony to the respect in which the Third Republic holds the author of the *Contrat Social*. The design is precisely what it should be. Philosophy, Truth, and Nature are surprised in a classic niche, while on either hand Fame and Music stand idly by. Nothing detracted from the superb irony of the event. The Third Republic is innocent of humour, as was Rousseau himself.

Thus in the name of the law reverence is paid to the father of Anarchy. Ravachol, Henri, Bonnot, and the other Apaches, Rousseau's unconscious disciples, have brandished their Brownings and thrown their bombs in vain. They have died some of them, with the Anarch's sentiments in their hearts, with the Anarch's words upon their lips, and Philosophy and Truth guard his image without a smile. And the voices of the few who uttered a protest sound as the voices of men crying in the wilderness to the ears of modern France.

The reason why the views of Rousseau are acceptable to the democrats of to-day is that he was the apotheosis of the half-baked. For wit and learning he had a profound contempt. He had read Plutarch and La Calprenède, and little else. He tried all the modern institutions, which he discussed, by the test of Lycurgus, in his eyes a real and moving personage. To the other lessons of history he turned a deaf ear. His intelligence was warped and scanty. He was almost incapable of reason. And therefore, like many another sanguine person, he believed that he could solve by a gesture the many problems of life and policy. Of the catch-words which mean nothing, and yet have the power to inflame ill-balanced minds, he was the facile master. ' Man is born free,' said he, ' and everywhere he is in chains.' The sentence has a lofty, generous sound, and contains all the seeds of error. No man is born free. If he were, he would never live to lie in a cradle. We are enslaved from our birth by helplessness, law, and custom. Such freedom as we win, we win in our manhood by wisdom and energy. But Truth, which now guards his monument, was never of interest to Rousseau, who lived in his sensations, and believed that whatever he felt for the moment was beyond the reach of argument.

The wonderful discourse which won him the prize at Dijon, and which piqued the curiosity of the fashionable world, was firmly based on ignorance and confusion of thought. The inspiration of it came to him on a summer day, when he was walking at

Vincennes.   Suddenly a thousand images convinced
him that man, good naturally, had been made bad by
institutions.   The comparison, which should have
preceded this conclusion, was beyond the reach of
Rousseau.   He knew nothing of savage man, whom
he set up as an ideal.   He knew nothing of the stages
through which man had passed before he had arrived
at the civilisation of the eighteenth century.   He was
sublimely unconscious of the world that lay about
him.   But he had found his thesis.

A flood of rhetoric overwhelmed him on that
summer day at Vincennes, and the rest was easy.
His discourse, moreover, was well fitted to catch the
popular ear.   A Society, which had sacrificed too
much to artificial refinement, was delighted to play
with the idea of savagery. It did not take Rousseau
as seriously as Rousseau took himself ; it liked to
babble of green fields under its powdered wigs, and to
twist nature itself into a kind of artifice.   Rousseau
was content, because he thought he had struck a blow
at civilisation, that he had defeated for ever the armed
forces of tradition.   Of course, he deceived himself.
Tradition is as strong to-day as ever it was, in spite of
his assaults.   His influence has been felt only by those
as ignorant and sentimental as himself.   And great as
this influence has seemed in time of stress, it has been
intermittent.   A mere breath of reaction checks, the
lightest consideration of history dispels it.   It is not
worth a grave discussion.   Voltaire's light-hearted
comment on the Discourses is final.   ' Never was

such cleverness used,' said he, 'for the mere purpose of making us all stupid. As I read your book I longed to walk on all-fours. But as I have lost the habit for more than sixty years, I feel, unhappily, that it is impossible to resume it.' The human race also has lost the habit, and is not likely to resume it at the persuasion of Rousseau or of any one else.

Rousseau, then, had no system of political philosophy, no settled design of reform. The Socialists and the Anarchists, men at the opposite poles of thought, may use his platitudes with equal pertinence to justify their excesses. His works were a gospel to the Jacobins; his dangerous maxims shed a vast deal of blood in the Revolution; and there are many demagogues to-day who mistake the stale echoes of Rousseau for their own inventions. That his doctrines have persisted here and there is not wholly strange. A vague sentimentality is always sure of a hearing. And then the scandal of his life, by far the best material of his books, saves him from oblivion to-day, as once it made him fashionable. If we may believe him, there was no meanness of which he was not capable. Were half his *Confessions* true, a more cravenly despicable man never lived upon the earth. Candour alone redeems his vices, and candour is not enough. And not merely was he sentimental and shameless. Above and before all things, he was superbly eloquent. The gift of persuasion is still in his dead words. Bitterly as he affected to despise the graces of literary style, it is to these very graces

that he owes his immortality.   In the field of natural,
flowing rhetoric he was, and remains, invincible.
Not even the evil that has always followed in his train
can blind us to the noble artistry of his prose.

There is no greater danger to the State than sentimentality, except eloquence, and Rousseau had the
double gift.   He used it in literature, as he used it
in controversy.   He displays it in his *Confessions*, the
book of all his books which has the best chance of
life.   He believed that in composing this he stood
alone.   ' I am attempting an enterprise,' he said, ' in
which I have no example, and in which I shall have
no imitator.   I wish to show to my like a man in
all the truth of his nature, and this man shall be me.
Moi seul.'   Here he deceived himself.   He did but
follow Montaigne for an example, and his imitators
are like the sands of the sea for number.   At all points
the advantage is with Montaigne, whose portraiture
of himself has a largeness and breadth of style, as well
as a sanity of perception, to which Rousseau could
never attain.   Montaigne saw himself, so to say,
in relation to Plutarch's heroes.   He measured his
thoughts and his feelings, his vices and virtues, by the
experience of the greatest.   His egoism is steeped in
antiquity, and is coloured by the past.   Rousseau
never lets you lose sight of his littleness.   His world
is designed upon a petty scale.   The man who records
that he threw a false suspicion of theft upon a servant-
maid is almost worse than he who committed the sin.
By his selection you know him and condemn.   Yet

even in condemnation you admire.   He was wayward,
greedy, unscrupulous, quarrelsome, indecent.   For
him knowledge was smattering ; his opinions were
dark with error.   'Too many honest men would
be wrong,' said Diderot, 'if Jean-Jacques were
right.'   In brief, he was the sentimentalist of genius,
who wrote the *Confessions*, and who, less than any
Frenchman that ever was born, deserved a pompous
monument in the Panthéon.

CHAMFORT

NICOLAS CHAMFORT sums up, in his life and in his prose, what was good and evil in the France of the eighteenth century. A nameless wanderer, who knew not his father, he was still a finished courtier. A cynic in temper, he fell into Jacobinism from a profound contempt of King, Court, and Government. The sycophant who said on the death of Louis XIV., 'after the death of the King, one can believe anything,' was highly despicable to his mind. He could not shut his eyes to the folly of Ministers. 'Without the Government,' he wrote, 'there would be no more laughter in France.' Yet no sooner did Jacobinism find its logical conclusion in the Terror than he hated those who had been his colleagues. He translated the foolish legend 'Fraternity or Death' into 'Be my brother, or I kill you.' 'The fraternity of these rascals,' said he in an imperishable phrase, 'is the fraternity of Cain and Abel.'

The Jacobins rewarded him after their kind. He was a philosopher, not a butcher, and so they flung him into prison. His free soul could not bear the restraint. 'It is not life; it is not death,' said he, 'and there is nothing between. I must open my eyes

upon the heavens or close them in the tomb.' He
was set at liberty, and then again his unbridled tongue
offended the scoundrels. A second time the
assassins came for him, and he had sworn to die rather
than return to his dungeon. A pistol-shot half
killed him ; he seized a razor and did his best to cut
his throat. It was a poor attempt, and a friend
found him bathed in blood and guarded by a gendarme.
Not even in this supreme humiliation did his wit
desert him. 'You see,' said he, 'what it is to be
clumsy. I can't succeed, even in killing myself.'
He had perforated an eye instead of blowing out his
brains ; he had scarred his breast, when he had
meant to pierce his heart. 'The truth is,' said he,
'I thought of Seneca, and in his honour I wished
to open a vein ; but he was rich, he had his desire :
a very hot bath and all his comforts. I am a poor devil,
and I am still here ; but I have a bullet in my head—
that is the chief thing, and sooner or later there is an
end.' He kept his gay courage to his death. 'At
last I am leaving this world,' he murmured to Sieyès,
'where you must break your heart or bronze it.'

Chamfort, in truth, was born and died a wit, and
a wit could not hope to escape the fury of the blood-
thirsty pedants who made the Revolution. 'Ready
wit,' wrote Chesterfield to his son, who needed not
the caution, 'may create many admirers ; but, take
my word for it, makes few friends. It shines and
dazzles, like the noonday sun ; but, like that too, is
very apt to scorch.' There was a peculiar danger in

Chamfort's wit, which scorched them most fiercely who knew no other punishment for those with whom they disagreed than the guillotine. Driven into Jacobinism, as I have said, by contempt of the Court, he did not spare the follies of the people. ' The public, the public ! ' he exclaimed. ' How many fools does it take to make a public ? ' The public avenged the insult with its customary brutality. And if Chamfort's wit was the clear cause of his death, at least he was spared one dishonour. His fame has not been outraged by travesties of his conversation. The ancient sayings of fools have not been carelessly ascribed to him. For so careful was he of his reputation that he gathered together his own witticisms, he edited his own table-talk. In his *Caractères et Portraits*, and still more lucidly in his *Maximes et Pensées*, you may discover his opinions and catch an echo of his wit. In style he belongs to the great tradition. He is of the race of La Bruyère and La Rochefoucauld. None but an accomplished Frenchman ever packed so much sense in so small a space. His is the true economy of speech which wastes no word, and yet is never obscure. He is restless, cynical, full of contempt for the human race. How could he have been otherwise, living and suffering when he did ?

The epoch of the Revolution was not an epoch of cold reflection and judicial summaries. Chamfort saw those about him with a keen eye, and described them with a mordant pen. ' There are more fools

than wise men,' he wrote, 'and even in the wise men
there is more folly than wisdom.' His own career
had taught him that neither riches nor poverty could
save a man's soul. Independence was the one thing
needful. 'Prejudice, vanity, calculation,' said he,
'they are what governs the world. He who knows
no other rule of conduct than reason, truth, and sentiment has nothing in common with Society. It is in
himself that he must seek and find all his happiness.'
Never did a man match practice with theory more
closely than did Chamfort. Such happiness as he
enjoyed he found in himself, and his maxims are
nothing more than his own bitter experience, expressed
in epigram.

Society for him was a mere resort of folly.
'Watching what takes place in the world,' he wrote,
'the worst of misanthropes must end in gaiety, and
Heraclitus himself die of laughter.' And who, in
this sorry farce of life, shall escape the bitter smile of
scorn? 'Few men understand,' he thought, 'how
much wit they need to avoid appearing ridiculous.'
And, if he demanded wit in others, perhaps for
this very reason he was the declared enemy of prigs
and pedants. 'There are some noble qualities,' said
he, 'which render their possessors unfit for society.
You don't go to market with ingots, but with silver
and small change.' It irked him always to carry the
burden of life, and his attempt at suicide, if clumsy,
was logical. 'He who learns to know the evils of
nature,' said he, 'despises death. He who learns to

know the evils of Society despises life.' Yet even
life need not make us despair. 'To live is a malady,
of which sleep relieves us every sixteen hours; it is
a palliative : death is the remedy.' And again :
'There are two things to which we must submit, if
we would not find life insupportable : the injuries
of time, and the injustice of men.'

His philosophy is not gay. The moment at
which Cain and Abel illustrated the virtue of brother-
hood was not apt for smiles. Yet when, as in his
Caractères et Portraits, he painted the wit of others,
he winged his shaft with gaiety. In these swift
sketches he resumed the thought of Rousseau and
Voltaire, Diderot and Helvétius. He proved himself,
so to say, the Joe Miller of the intellect. True, his
specimens of wit are not all of equal value. He
himself was conscious of the temptation which beset
him. 'The collectors of *bons mots*,' said he, ' resemble
those who eat cherries or oysters ; they choose the
best first and end by eating all.' And though he might
have been sterner in rejection, he put together a book
which it is still pleasant to read, and which reflects
with a humorous fidelity the wit of the Salons.
Above all, his life and work were singularly uniform.
With the same light-hearted cynicism wherewith he
unpacked upon paper his general contempt of Court
and people, he faced an uncomfortable death, the
poor reward of candour and understanding.

S

MIRABEAU

THE difficulties which interrupt painting Mirabeau's picture are artistic rather than historical. There is no lack of apposite material, nor are there any haunting mysteries in the career of this man, who lived in the glare of publicity. There is every temptation to spoil the portrait by prejudice or exaggeration. Mirabeau designed his own life with so great a purpose, he demanded so vast a theatre for his performances, that it is not easy, even after a hundred and fifty years, to see him in a right relation to his world. Moreover, his double character has confused the superficial observer, who cannot conceive the subtle shades which separate black from white. For, truly, Mirabeau was neither white nor black ; devil and angel, he was Catiline tempered by Gracchus, an heroic mixture of public virtue and private vice, the Wilkes-Chatham of Macaulay's witty phrase. In brief, Mirabeau's faults were many and obvious ; nor did the statesman himself attempt to conceal them. They were discussed assiduously during his lifetime, and since his death they have obscured the manifold good he achieved, or might have achieved, had fortune and reputation favoured him. But Mirabeau, after all, was eminent for a statesmanship, unique in his

time ; and it is for this, as well as for his superb, unconscious gift of drama, that he is wisely remembered.

When Mirabeau, at the age of eight-and-twenty,
was imprisoned at Vincennes, he increased his stature
during the confinement by three inches. And this
story gives us the only reasonable clue to his character
and temperament. He was abnormal in all things ;
he surpassed his fellows in energy and unscrupulousness, in repulsion and in charm, in intellect and in
folly. A glance at Houdon's bust will reveal the
man more vividly than volumes of biography. For
although the sculptor angrily repudiated the desire of
packing thought into marble or bronze, he could not
but display in this mottled face something of Mirabeau's
rugged force and vivid mutability. Indeed, Mirabeau
was changeable as the sea, and neither his father nor
his uncle, who watched over his youth with suspicion,
could ever make up his mind whether the boy was
destined for saint or sinner. His father insisted that
he was plastic as sand, and ready to take upon himself
any impression whatever, if only it were fleeting.
His uncle declared that ' if not worse than Nero he
will be better than Marcus Aurelius ' ; all confessed
that at five he was the wonder of Paris ; and, as he
came to manhood, not even his prodigious vices
hindered the growth of his fearless intelligence.

His father, who shirked the responsibility of education, thought imprisonment the best of discipline, and
the young Mirabeau wandered from one dungeon to
another. The punishment was never irksome, since

his amazing geniality converted the harshest gaoler into a devoted slave. So passionate a lover could hardly make a patient husband, and with his marriage the serious troubles of his life began. His love of pleasure and display brought him speedily to bankruptcy, and he had only been married fifteen months when he owed 200,000 livres, had pawned his wife's jewels, and had begun to cut down his ancestral timber. Then came the elopement with Sophie de Monnier, which was expiated by a term of imprisonment at Vincennes; and thus Mirabeau undertook to save his country with a heavier weight of indiscretions upon his shoulders than the most upright statesman could sustain.

'What could I not have done,' said he, 'had I come to the States-General with the reputation of Malesherbes.' Alas! his was not the reputation of Malesherbes, and even the turbulent spirits of the Revolution distrusted him. Nevertheless, in statesmanship he was always upright. As Romilly said, his ambition was of the noblest kind; only he was unscrupulous about the means of gratifying this noble ambition. Money was the first necessity of his life; he must live in palaces, and enjoy the splendour of reckless luxury. Wherefore he was compelled to accept payment from the King, or from whomsoever showed an open hand. But he was never bought; he did no more than let himself be paid; that, says Sainte-Beuve, is the distinction; and it is no wonder that the distinction was too fine for the discernment of contemporary eyes.

The worst is that Mirabeau's imperious necessities
rendered his political sagacity of no effect. He was
wholly sincere in his devotion to France, and in his
aspirations after better government. And few would
put their trust in his sincerity. When once his rapacity
was satisfied, he was prepared to show himself a single-
minded politician. He could not conceal the extrava-
gances of his passions, and all the world suspected a
tortuous cunning in his most valiant action. His
unsurpassed eloquence should have dominated the
Assembly ; his perfect mastery of political truth should
have convinced the most obdurate ; his sense of stage
effect should have dazzled even his enemies. He
was cast aside for such men as Necker and Lafayette,
whom he despised, and it was without a touch of
hypocrisy that he deplored 'the great injury the
irregularities of his youth had inflicted on the commonwealth.' His temperament drove him instantly to
convert thought into action. 'It is my fatal
destiny,' he complained, 'to do all things in twenty-
four hours.' His superhuman efforts were of no
avail ; in vain did he accomplish the work of ten
heroes. 'I shall die,' said he to Dumont, 'before
anything is accomplished ; perhaps we shall not meet
again. . . . The Members of the Assembly have
wished to govern the King, instead of wishing to
govern through him, but soon neither he nor they will
govern.' The words were prophetic in all senses.
After a three days' debate and a reckless orgy, Mirabeau attended the Assembly to protect the interests

of his friend La Marck. He spoke at great length, and gave up to friendship the poor remnant of his life. Carried back to La Marck, 'your case is won,' he murmured, 'but I am dying.' Thereupon he composed himself for an heroic scene, and truly, as Talleyrand said, no man ever dramatised his death to better effect. 'Well, my dear critic of courageous deaths,' said he to La Marck, 'are you satisfied?' And to Frochot he exclaimed with a smile, 'Yes, raise that head; would that I could bequeath it to you!' Would that he could, indeed! For with Mirabeau the statesmanship of France was eclipsed, since Mirabeau was the one man who might have saved his country from the reign of terror, and replaced wanton destruction by wise reform.

WILLIAM WINDHAM

IT was an unkind irony of fate which drove
William Windham into the service of his
country. In a letter to Mrs. Crewe he once described
himself as ' a politician among scholars and a scholar
among politicians.' By those who did not perceive
the close consistency of his career he was known as
the Weathercock, and he deserved the dishonouring
name no more than Halifax deserved to be ridiculed
as the Trimmer. Though he gave himself freely to
what he believed to be a public duty, he never seemed
at his ease in politics. As his friend Malone said, he
' was not what is called a thorough party-man,' and
though a Whig by preference he did not adopt the Whig
creed that nothing was of the smallest importance
except office. He was therefore harassed throughout
his life by a kind of remorse. ' There seem to be
but two modes of life to be followed with any satisfaction,' he wrote, ' military and literary. The
management of civil affairs, depending, as they do,
on the consent of others, is liable to be thwarted at
every step by their sordidness and folly, and is the most
thankless employment of all. I am sick of the world,
and dissatisfied, though not for anything I have done
in the way of publick conduct.'

Born in 1750, William Windham resisted the call of politics until he was three-and-thirty, and then with much misgiving he accepted the post of Chief Secretary to the Lord-Lieutenant of Ireland. When he confided his fears to Dr. Johnson, ' Don't be afraid, sir,' said that eminent man, ' you will soon make a very pretty rascal.' Unhappily for his peace of mind, he had not in him the seeds of rascality. Distrust of himself and too keen a sensibility persuaded him to resign in a few months, and though he took part in the persecution of Warren Hastings, he might have retired to his books and his prize-fights and his bull-baitings had not the Revolution deluged France with blood.

In a moment his mind and heart were changed. He was transformed suddenly into as fierce an anti-Jacobin as Burke himself, his friend and master. Henceforth he had but one ambition—to combat the Revolution by all the means in his power. Though now and again he despaired, he never for one moment relented. ' All is dark and doubtful,' he wrote in 1790 ; ' nothing certain but death and taxes, and that Pitt will come out with new lustre from all the present measures and heap new confusions upon his oppositionists.' He was ready to serve under any leader who would regard France with untiring enmity, until a Bourbon again sat upon the throne. ' My hostility to Jacobinism and all its works,' he wrote, ' weak or wicked, is more steady and strong than ever. If Pitt is the man by whom this must be opposed,

Pitt is the man whom I shall stand by.' When the Duke of Portland and the other Whigs rallied to Pitt's side, Windham took office with them, and he for one was quite ready to drop for a while his Whiggish tactics. The first Whig, said Dr. Johnson, was the devil. The first and last and all the Whigs between were placemen, and it was but natural that the Duke of Portland should think the safety of England an insignificant trifle compared with the appointment of Fitzwilliam to the Lord-Lieutenancy of Ireland. It is to Windham's lasting credit that in this shabby intrigue he took no part. ' I say it with heartfelt anguish,' wrote Mansfield to him, ' my clear opinion is that, if there be a rupture at present, the country is undone.' And Windham agreed with him.

The mere hint of peace seemed to Windham a far worse calamity than a broken Government. So long as the war lasted he did not wholly despair of the commonwealth. ' The aspect of affairs is not good,' he wrote in 1800 ; ' but there does not appear any immediate prospect of peace (the blessings of peace), and that being the case there is still hope. In war a thousand things may happen, but peace once made, the power of Bonaparte seems certainly fixed, and I know not then how we are to escape. Everything is, however, very bad. One Emperor mad, another weak and pusillanimous. The King of Prussia governed by narrow, selfish, and short-sighted counsels ; no vigour, no energy, no greatness of plan but in the French, and they accordingly govern everything.' A miserable confession for an anti-Jacobin to make.

The peace of Amiens broke his heart. After this treachery, as he deemed it, he could never trust any of his leaders again. 'I can have no idea of the measure in question,' he wrote to Addington when the 'dreadful intelligence' of peace was brought to him, 'but as the commencement of a career which, by an easy descent, and step by step, but at no very distant period, will conduct the country to a situation where, when it looks at last for its independence, it will find that it is already gone. I have no idea how the effect of this measure is ever to be recovered. Chance may do much, but, according to any conception I can form, the country has received its death blow.' We can only regret that this loyal champion of law and order did not live to see the crowning mercy of Waterloo.

William Windham was something more than a mere politician. He was a great English gentleman, according to the wise interpretations of his time. He had a natural love of polite letters, and might, perhaps, have been eminent in science. Though many objections may be made to his war policy, his courage was undoubted. Not content to sit at home and devise plans of campaign, he thought it consistent with his duty to follow the army and show himself in the trenches. With still greater courage he urged upon Pitt the recall of the Duke of York from a command for which he was obviously unfit, and the letters which set forth his reasons are documents of great value. And being an English gentleman, he opposed with what force he might ' the rearing of puritanism into a system.' He defended what he would have called ' the manly sport of bull-baiting ' with an energy which Cobbett and Canning could not surpass. He was, besides, a constant patron of the prize-ring. It is characteristic of both men that Lord Grey should close a letter addressed to Windham, and denouncing Bonaparte, with a comment upon a famous fight. ' I was very sorry for Belcher's defeat,' wrote Grey, ' though I do not know why I should prefer him to the Chicken except that he has lost an eye. I admire the Chicken's generosity, and I hope Cobbett, who is so warm an advocate of the good cause, will not neglect the ace that is to be made out of it.'

Such, a century ago, was the wholesome tradition of politics.

LANDOR ON FOX

LANDOR'S Commentary upon Charles James Fox is a literary curiosity. Of the original edition only one copy is known to have survived—the copy which Landor himself gave to Southey. That John Murray should have declined to publish it in 1812 is not remarkable. The attack upon Canning, as unjust as it is fierce, could not have been passed by the proprietor of *The Quarterly Review*, and Landor refused Murray's offer to transfer the book to another publisher. So, for almost a century, it was kept from us.

Gifford described the book as Jacobinical, and a Jacobin Landor was, with an aristocratic love of polite literature. There was no politician of his day that he did not assail with a majestic violence. Pitt, in his eyes, was a scoundrel, by whose infamous policy the clay idol of France had been cast in solid gold. Canning 'was a very extraordinary boy, and is a very extraordinary boy still. He has not grown an inch in intellect ; he has, however, given one sure and unequivocal proof of his abilities in making Lord Castlereagh popular for several days—as long a time as Lord Castlereagh was ever thought of.' In brief, all are bad, but by far the worst is the man whose professions were the highest—Charles James Fox.

The Life of Fox, by one Trotter, which served as the text of Landor's Commentary, is long since forgotten. It is the work of a henchman who approached his hero on bended knee and with cap in hand, who, writing of the people's champion, proved by his obsequious attitude that he never harboured the superstition of equality in his grateful breast. And the Commentary suffers in interest from the paltriness of its excuse. Moreover, since 1812 the popular opinion of Fox has undergone a vast change. There are few critics of history left who believe that Fox, the sentimental rhetorician and intrepid gamester, could in any circumstances have been the saviour of his country, or would, had he been able, have raised a little finger for his country's salvation. However, in 1812 Fox was still a legend—a legend which Landor set himself sedulously to discredit. To Landor, friend of 'freedom' as he was, Fox's apostasy was unpardonable, and he denounces it with all the energy of his clear-cut style. Fox 'never came into office,' says he, 'but through a breach of honour, never without a close and intimate coalition with men whom he had frequently, and loudly, and justly denounced as worthy of the gallows. So atrocious is his guilt, he never joined them but at the very moment when their criminality was at its highest ; and when, without his coalescence, the people would have dragged them to punishment or abandoned them to disgrace.' Landor's interpretation of facts will not always bear criticism. There is no doubt as to the strength of his advocacy.

For Fox's private character Landor had but a light esteem. He allows him to have been amiable, and that is all. 'In the times of the Curii and Camilli,' he writes, 'Mr. Fox would have been a prodigy of abomination. In those of Charles II. he would have appeared one of the brightest and best courtiers. He came forward into life with every advantage, and the age was neither too light nor too dark a background for the clear and steady exhibition of his features. He found no fault with the luxuries of this nation, and was deeply imbued with that portion of its commercial spirit which exacts no industry and pays no tax—the aristocratical commerce of the gaming-table.' Every statement which Trotter makes in Fox's favour Landor counters with unfailing vigour. Says Trotter: 'Although Fox saw the ruin prepared by a rash and obstinate Minister, no expression of bitterness ever escaped his lips.' To which Landor contemptuously replies: 'No more than against his opponents at cards. If he lost to-night he might win to-morrow.' When Trotter describes the youth of Fox as 'warm and impetuous,' he provokes the commentator's bitterest scorn. 'Fox's youth was very well known,' writes Landor, 'to have exceeded in every kind of profligacy the youth of any Englishman his contemporary. To the principles of a Frenchman he added the habits of a Malay in idleness, drunkenness and

gaming.' This is true enough, but if only Fox
had been what Landor thought a true friend of liberty,
he would have looked with a gentle and kindly eye
upon his habits and his principles.

In truth, you read this Commentary, not for the
sake of Fox, but for the sake of Landor. If Landor's
politics are a piece of mere prejudice, if his reading of
history is obscure and perplexed, the genius of the
writer is stamped upon every page. The style is as
bright as crystal and as hard. Its energy does not
flag for a single line, and it belongs so intimately to
the man himself, that, as you read, you seem to hear
the echo of a human voice. Southey's eulogy is not
pitched in too high a key. ' Your prose,' he wrote
to Landor, ' is as much your own as your poetry.
There is a life and vigour in it to which I know no
parallel. It has the poignancy of champagne, and
the body of English October. Neither you nor
Murray gave me any hint that the " Commentary "
was yours, but I could not look into these pages without knowing that it could not be the work of any other
man.' And the form in which the Commentary is
cast gives it a personal character, which a grave essay
would lack. It has the quickness and brilliance
of table-talk. Landor disagrees bitterly with the
biographer. He has a lively repartee, always ready
for Trotter's panegyric, and it need not be said that
he always gets the better of the discussion

STENDHAL'S *NAPOLEON*

WHEN Stendhal sat down, a year after Waterloo, to begin his *Life of Napoleon*, he might claim many qualifications for the task. He had seen, known, and spoken with his hero. He had lived at his Court ; he had followed him in his wars ; he had shared in the administration of the countries which he conquered ; he had enjoyed for many years the intimacy of one among the most influential of his Ministers. He saw him for the first time two days after his passage of Mount St. Bernard ; he was in his box at the Scala on the morrow of the victory of Marengo ; he watched his triumphal entry into Berlin in 1806 ; and he shared the hardships of the retreat from Moscow. He wrote, therefore, with the authority of one who had known and admired. His sympathy grew with the years. He was convinced that the more light which was thrown upon Napoleon's career the greater he would appear. A love for Napoleon he confessed to be the only passion left him, but this love never hindered him from seeing the faults of his hero's character, and the weaknesses wherewith he was justly reproached.

And Stendhal's manner was perfectly adapted to his enterprise. None knew better than he that great

288

actions stand in no need of great words.   He had
not, as he said, any pretence to a fine style ; he held
emphasis in detestation, as the cousin of hypocrisy,
the fashionable vice of the nineteenth century.   He
warned his readers that they would find in his pages
' no grand phrases, no style that burns the paper,
no dead bodies.'   By him, at any rate, the words
' horrible, sublime, terror, execrable, the dissolution
of Society ' are never used.   He might seem crude,
and crudity he confessed was a fault of style.   Of
hypocrisy, a fault of morals, he was never guilty, and
thus it was that, knowledge and temperament aiding,
he was able to sketch upon paper a vivid and truthful
portrait of Napoleon the Great.

Born out of due time, compelled to witness the
beginnings of the Romantic Movement, which he
despised, Stendhal was before all'things a psychologist.
He once said that he learned to write in order that
he might forget it.   He never lost his keen insight
into character, and it is this insight which gives a
superb interest to his study of Napoleon.   He did
not set out to write a history of France.   Events did
not engross him, except so far as they lit up a dark
place in Napoleon's career.   It is upon the man that
the eye of his mind is perpetually fixed.   In the sternly
Italian character of Madame Lætitia he found the
clue to the mystery of her son.   Napoleon, in fact,
was an Italian—an Italian, if you will, of the fifteenth
century—who thought with strength, who reasoned
with the closest logic, and who knew but the briefest

T

interval between thought and deed. He entertained
no project save with passion, a passion followed always
by moments of absolute weariness and disgust, which
violently agitated his Italian nature, the complete
antithesis to the reasonable souls of Washington,
Lafayette, and William III. Whatever he achieved
was the triumph of character rather than of knowledge.
Stendhal declares that, though Napoleon had read
and forgotten much, his education was incomplete.
' Except mathematics, artillery, and the military art
of Plutarch,' says the biographer, ' he knew nothing.'
And to no man did ignorance matter less. In
ordinary intercourse he never betrayed it, for it was
his privilege always to direct conversation, and he
permitted no discussion which might expose his lack
of knowledge.

As Paoli said, Napoleon was cast in an antique
mould ; he was a man of Plutarch. The ample
simplicity of word and act which belonged to the
heroic age was instinctive in him, and was enhanced
by the study of Livy's *Roman History* and the *Parallel
Lives*, which were the catechism of his boyhood.
It was enough for him to cherish the dominant
emotions of the period, to be useful to the fatherland,
and to pursue glory. And it was only by the help
of the sword that he could pursue glory or serve the
fatherland. Stendhal is quick to recognise that the
Italian campaign was the masterpiece of Napoleon's
life, and he makes no attempt to dim that masterpiece
by praising the Code or the Decree of Moscow.

He loved the military virtues as ardently as his hero loved them.   He saw clearly that they were the only virtues which, in an age of universal hypocrisy, hypocrisy itself could not profitably replace, and he regretted that Napoleon ever left the command of his army to sit upon an Emperor's throne.

For Stendhal shares the regret of Madame Lætitia that Napoleon claimed for himself the dignities and splendours of a sovereign.   And his regret is the more sincere because it springs from no superficial love of equality.   Stendhal desired no more than ' the maintenance of what is ' ;   he did not permit his political religion to cloud his judgment.   He admitted that Napoleon lied, when he wrote as an Emperor, when he did not permit the heart of the great man to break through the Imperial crust.   Lying, in fact, he believed to be Napoleon's dominant vice, lying for a purpose.   He lied at St. Helena, says Stendhal, because he was preparing a throne for the King of Rome, because he was inventing his own legend. And it was this refusal to see things as they were that Stendhal thinks was Napoleon's undoing.   He did not fall by hate, as so many great men fall.   His biographer declares that he never hated anybody except a Jacobin.   This is not strictly true.   He hated also the English, the journalists, and Mme. de Staël. Nevertheless, it was deception rather than hate that undid him.   He believed falsely that he could unite in himself the two offices of Emperor and Commander-in-Chief.   He believed, still more falsely, that he

could govern Europe with the help of the mediocrities
who surrounded him.   In other words, like many
another man of genius, he could bear the presence of
none save the flatterer, and he easily beguiled himself
that all the flatterer's tales were true.

Stendhal was confident that the *Life of Napoleon*
would be written once and for always in 1860 or 1880.
He did not foresee the activity of the book-makers.
Vast libraries have already been dedicated to the eluci-
dation of Napoleon and his character.   He has been
set upon a thousand pedestals ; he has been looked
at from every quarter of the heavens.   We have
been told, àt intolerable length, how he behaved to
women, with what eye he envisaged art, what were
his true plan and sense of justice.   He has long lain
buried beneath a vast heap of military details and civil
facts.   Talleyrand has exhausted his ingenuity to
prove that he was ruined because he refused to take
his advice.   Metternich has shown to his own satisfaction that Napoleon was a ruffian who did not
understand the proper treatment of ambassadors.
The printed monument of St. Helena grows ever
higher, not that Napoleon may shine with a purer
effulgence, but that another trait of contempt may be
put upon Hudson Lowe, the mere instrument of
other men's decrees, who has no claim to the eminence
thrust upon him, of an aunt sally.   And every step
in the path of superfluous research carries us further
and further from Napoleon.   For which reason,
among others, it is well to turn back again to Stendhal's

' fragments,' which have no other object than to show the man and not events, to give to biography the only meaning which an artist can find for it.   For whatever his deficiencies may have been, Stendhal possessed at least the genius of omission, and knew that no worse stumbling-block can trip the biographer than a mass of unimpeachable and disrelated facts.